Praise for Axis

"I wish there were 100s of groups like Axis. We are losing the next generation. We need help from people like Axis to reach teenagers."

Tim Keller, PhD, Author & Pastor

"I applaud the way Axis communicates to young people and parents. They are deeply in touch with student culture and trends. Masterful job."

Kara Powell, PhD, Author, & Director of Fuller Youth Institute

While praying over the Axis Cofounders Ravi prayed, "We are living in a world of such havoc. How wonderful to see a bright light beginning to shine in a dark place. Axis' calling is to serve families. May God give them the joy of seeing that vision fulfilled, because it is pleasing in God's eyes and glorifying to Him."

Ravi Zacharias, Founder of RZIM & Renowned Evangelist

"I find the work of Axis relevant and insightful as a parent and as a researcher on demographic trends. Our team has read your columns with great interest finding many of the same trends in our research."

Brooke Hempell, SVP Research, Barna Global

"Axis is made up of young people reaching young people. Axis resources are relevant and speak to teens' hearts."

Jim Daly, President of Focus on the Family

"Axis is more effective than any group I know in confronting student apathy."

John Stonestreet, Colson Center President & Breakpoint Host

"Axis is on the cutting edge of training students and parents how to think biblically about culture, media, and technology."

Sean McDowell, PhD, Professor, Speaker, Author

"Axis is a mature and unified group who can be trusted to hear from God. I love that they're solution-focused. They don't like data for the sake of data. They correctly use it to ask and answer the right and hard questions to provide solutions that parents, grandparents, educators, and pastors need."

Kathy Koch, PhD, Founder and President, Celebrate Kids, Inc.

"Axis is a ministry that I endorse & support because they are an equipping ministry—equipping not just students, but the critical leadership elements around them: teachers, parents & grandparents."

Del Tackett, PhD, Architect of The Truth Project

"I highly recommend Axis. They get the conversation going in a way that reaches the hearts of everyone in the school community—staff, teachers, parents, grandparents and students."

Jeff Myers, PhD, President of Summit Ministries

"After hosting a daily radio program, FamilyLife Today, for over a quarter century, I've had the privilege of featuring over a thousand guests on every imaginable subject. As I was writing The Art of Parenting, *I decided I'd ask one of these guests, David Eaton, to write a chapter about developing your child's character with regard to technology. David heads up Axis, one of the most effective and relevant organizations already in this arena. I asked the Axis team of twenty-somethings to create 'uranium' for parents. It was better than uranium, it was PLUTONIUM!"*

Dennis Rainey, CEO of FamilyLife, FamilyLife Today Host

Smartphone Sanity

A proven plan to protect your kids, build trust, and bring smartphone balance to your home.

By David Eaton, Jeremiah Callihan,
and the Axis Team, with Sarah Miles

Smartphone Sanity: A proven plan to protect your kids, build trust, and bring smartphone balance to your home.

By David Eaton, Jeremiah Callihan,
and the Axis Team, with Sarah Miles

Axis
PO BOX 63572, Colorado Springs, CO 80962
www.axis.org

ISBN: 978-1-7334591-2-9
Ebook ISBN: 978-1-7334591-1-2

Cover Design: Brent Hammett brenthammett.com

Edited by Sarah Miles: kilnliterary.com

Printed in the United States of America

Dedication

To the incredible parents and grandparents who are daily guiding and raising the next generation. We are amazed by you. Hang in there!

Also, special thanks to the awesome dad who gave this book its name (He happens to have a teenage daughter that he speaks with frequently about her smartphone!)

Contents

Start

Step 1: Refocus

Step 2: Dangers

Step 3: Boundaries

Step 4: Make A Plan

End

START

1. The Catastrophe that Caused this Book

I (David) was stumped. I had just finished a rather explosive discussion about the limits a parent was placing on their teen's phone when that teen snapped: *"The stricter the parent, the sneakier the child."*

What a zinger. In that moment I was at a loss for words, and to be quite honest, that was the parting shot to a conversation that was an utter failure. The young lady was in my youth group (yes, I'm a part-time youth pastor as well as an Axis Cofounder) and she was furious with her mother. Nothing I said seemed to break through to her and I found myself very ill-equipped to talk about smartphones. I didn't have a context for how to help her (or her mom), and the moral of the story is that the young lady ended up getting two iPhones—one to use at her mom's house and the other to be used at her dad's house. Instead of trust being built, it was being unraveled.

This story was not the only parent/teen smartphone fight we had witnessed. As one dad stated to us, "I spend over $3,000 a year on my family's screens and data plans only to get into a yelling match once a week with my kids." Another parent even asked me to appear in court as an expert witness in a court case regarding his teen's phone. It is clear the smartphone parenting challenge has become universal.

At Axis we were determined to find a way to help parents create boundaries on their teen's phone while building trust and winning their kid's heart. We started on a journey to unpack the different aspects of smartphone discipleship and we were shocked with how complex the phone issue really was. No wonder this is such a thorn in the side of families.

GRANDPA BOB SOLVES THE RIDDLE

So, what exactly is the sleight of hand behind the comment, "The stricter the parent the sneakier the child"? We've had a lot of discussions about it at Axis. It's like a magic trick with words. At first the statement feels true, then it seems false, and then you eventually realize there are some hidden assumptions behind the declaration.

So we started asking the wisest parents that we knew about it and Grandpa Bob held the key to unlocking its mystery. His answer to the stricter/sneakier riddle was: The issue here is not strictness, but trust.

He asked, *"Are you raising a sin concealer or a sin confessor?"* This teen was assuming, unbeknownst to her, that her parents didn't have her best interest at heart and, ultimately, that God didn't have her best interest at heart. So instead of pointing our index fingers at our son or daughter and saying, "You are being sneaky," we need to ask a deeper question. Does my kid believe that God's path is good? Do they believe that God's way leads to life, flourishing, joy, and meaning? As G. K. Chesterton said,

> *Are you raising a sin concealer or a sin confessor?*

> *The more I considered Christianity, the more I found that while it had established a rule and order, the chief aim of that order was to give room for good things to run wild.*

And if their index finger is pointed back at us, and they say with hot angry tears streaming down their cheeks, "You are being too strict!," it might be good to self-reflect: Do my kids know that I have their best interests at heart? Do they know I am safe, quick to forgive, and eager to reconcile?

THE MOST IMPORTANT (SMARTPHONE) CONVERSATION

"I've only had one real conversation with my dad" stated April, a millennial in her thirties. When we heard this we couldn't believe it. How can you only have one real conversation with your dad and . . . *how could this not be catastrophic?* The rising generation (aka your kid) is having thousands of "conversations" every week via their smartphone with their friends, social media influencers, and targeted advertising. If they only have one real conversation with you, no wonder the gospel and your values are lost in translation! And if you aren't discipling your child, trust us—everyone else is. However, April was not done with her statement. She smiled sweetly and continued, "I've only had one real conversation with my dad, *and we've never stopped having that one conversation.*"

April has had a thirty-year conversation with her dad and, from the looks of it, she and her dad are planning on having *one conversation* for the rest of their lives!

Yes, your child may have an eighteen-month conversation with a youth pastor, a four-year conversation with a favorite coach, or even a ten-year conversation with your pastor. But with you, their parent, they can have a sixty-year conversation! No one will ever be more influential than you. It's sociologically true, it's historically true, it's intuitive, and, *of course*, it's biblical.

This book will help you have hundreds of conversations with your kid about the incredibly creative, massively dangerous, and ever-evolving smartphone. But what's the most important smartphone conversation you can have? It's the *one conversation* that ebbs and flows daily with your kid. The smartphone is just a part of that *very* important "one conversation." Having a teenager is like having tech-support living in your home! This is great when the internet goes down, but terrible when you try to implement limits on their phone settings. Your kid needs your wisdom and you need their tech expertise. The smartphone could completely torpedo your family and be the greatest source of frustration, angst, and defeat in your parenting journey; or it could be the single best tool for discipling your kid.

This book will give you a proven plan to protect your kids, build trust, and bring smartphone balance into your home. Whether you're shopping for your kid's first phone or your kid has had a smartphone for years, this is the book for you.

You have what it takes! Let's get started.

“

I’ve only had one real conversation with my dad . . .

. . . and we've never stopped having that one conversation.

”

2. The Not-So-Hidden Gospel

Welcome to *Smartphone Sanity*! Congratulations on taking the next step toward transforming your family's smartphones from a source of distraction, confusion, and conflict, into one of unity and flourishing. By following this intentional path you'll have the tools to thrive as a smartphone family.

HOW TO EXPERIENCE *SMARTPHONE SANITY*

- We divided this book into four steps built around the Gospel, the story of Creation, Curse, Law, and Renewal.
- Each step will start with a reflection on Scripture and will be followed by a few short chapters designed to be practical. Each chapter ends with an experience you can lean into . . . or skip!
- Finally, each of the four steps end with a family activity meant to draw you closer to your kids and open avenues of conversation.[1]

“*We divided this book into four steps built around the Gospel: the story of Creation, Curse, Law, & Renewal.*”

[1] All you firstborns out there & wonderful Enneagrams #1: You have immaculately manicured to-do lists and you have the spiritual gift of feeling guilty if you aren't perfect. Please relax. This book is designed to be your servant. Yes, this book if full of things to do but feel free to skim or skip as needed. We are in your corner!

NO PRESSURE, REALLY.

If you are the parent of an 8 to 18 year old you are probably busy . . . and exhausted! Please don't feel stuck in this four step model. Use this book as a reference and skip to the parts that matter most, or just skim the whole book on your flight home from a work trip. **We are in your corner. No pressure!**[2]

STEP ONE: REFOCUS

Gospel: *Creation*
Step One is about God's very good *Creation* and how to *Refocus* the way we view the world and our phones. It is all about how God created the cosmos and called it very good.

Goal: *Identify how to win the smartphone conversation.*
Axis, you, and even your kid want you (the parent) to win in the smartphone conversation. REALLY! But not by taking over, shutting down opinions, and being the bad guy. You win by being *win*some, understanding the issues, learning how to talk so they will listen, AND learning how to listen so that they will talk.

STEP TWO: DANGER

Gospel: *Curse*
Step Two looks at the *Danger* and brokenness surrounding phones from the *Curse*. We will examine the curse, or the fall, of God's very good creation.

Goal: *Know yourself and the dangerous world of the smartphone.*
We approach this step in a unique way. We'll start with your own self-awareness, then we'll address the things that you're most afraid your kids could be exposed to on their phones. This step and the first step are the philosophical foundation for the final two steps, ***which will be extremely practical.***

STEP THREE: BOUNDARIES

Gospel: *Law*
Step Three explores a system of *Boundaries* and controls. In many ways, it is parallel to the *Law* that God gave the Israelites. Remember, the law

---

[2] Read the previous footnote. Especially if you are like me, a firstborn.

was never enough, therefore we will finish with Step Four.

Goal: *Understand all phone controls.*
Not only do we uncover ALL THE SNEAKS in this step we also dig into all the options (and there are a lot of them) for setting up your kid's phone. It'll be very technical, and you'll come back to these chapters again and again. Your kid's phone can be setup for success, and we'll give you the knowledge you'll need to do so.

STEP FOUR: MAKE A PLAN

Gospel: *Renewal*
Step Four looks at how to *Make A Plan* to implement the law through loving relationship made possible by the *Renewal* of Jesus. We will talk about growing in wisdom by creating a plan that meets the requirements and heart of the law.

Goal: *Family conversations that last a lifetime.*
The turning point of the whole book is for your family to come together around your individual and collective smartphone habits. Involving your kid in the decisions you make moving forward is key, but there will be some non-negotiables you will want to make clear. This power balance is key, and we'll spend this final step addressing the different issues you'll want to think through before having a family smartphone meeting. This will create short-term success while incentivizing long-term success. This final step is meant to give you the framework for a Family Smartphone Agreement that will help your kid grow into a mature, self-controlled, and wise smartphone-user. The destination is not parental fascism, but finding a path for your kid to walk so that they gain smartphone independence.

FAMILY PHONE AGREEMENT MEETING

This is the end of the book, but not the end of the line. Remember, these conversations are meant to last a lifetime! Looking forward, your family will have your first Family Phone Agreement Meeting, working toward short term and long term success!

Let's start the journey to Smartphone Sanity!

3. Start on the Right Foot

Now that you have an orientation of the structure of this book, let's look at how we should prepare our hearts. The Axis Team has compiled a list of "parenting postures" from our personal experiences and from great advice we've heard from speaking to over 240,000 students and parents in the last 13 years. Read through the postures and pick three to focus on and apply to your family interactions.

There's a reason why we're having you start with this. Chances are you haven't purchased this book because you just want to use it for yourself; you're jumping in because you see this as an area in which your whole family needs improvement. This means that, for your family to buy in, conversations need to come into play at some point.

To do this you *have to* evaluate yourself first, by assessing how you want to carry yourself as you lead these conversations with your spouse, your younger and older children, and anyone else that may end up being part of the big smartphone conversation you're entering into. Reminding yourself to stick to your three postures will smooth the road for the journey ahead, we promise.

Pick three of these to focus on and write them down somewhere you can see them. Maybe put them on your bathroom mirror, the dashboard of your car, or dare we say . . . the home screen of your phone!

1. BE READY WHEN THEY ARE READY

Your kid may beat you to the punch when it comes to connecting; so, be ready to connect when they are.

2. REMEMBER THEY ARE YOUNG ADULTS

Do you go golfing with the guys from the office? Go to the movies with the girls? Invite your kid to participate in "adult" activities so that they can practice and form good habits under your supervision.

3. LET THEM BE BORED

Boredom leads to creativity (and resilience!). Rather than allowing your kid to constantly be stimulated by screens, let them engage their imagination.

> *"Only boring people get bored." A favorite quote from my mother-in-law, who has never been bored a day in her life.*

4. DO WHAT THEY LOVE

Don't try to engage in deep conversation without first investing the time. Spend 10 minutes with your kid 3 times a week doing something they enjoy. When it comes time to go deep, they will go with you.

5. ENGAGE THE FAMILY UNIT

Do things that draw the whole family close, whether that is a weekly family outing or having family dinners. Remind all members, but especially teenagers, that they have a whole team that has their back.

6. REMEMBER YOUR KID'S INTELLIGENCE; THEIR OPINION IS VALID, THOUGH NOT NECESSARILY RIGHT

While respect is earned, you can instill great habits in your kid by expecting intelligence from them. Show them that you care about their opinion and that their thoughts and opinions are valuable; however, also explain that their opinion may not be correct and that it is okay to not always be right.

7. BE HUMBLE

Your kid knows things you don't know, and that is okay. Always approach your kid with humility, recognizing your own mistakes and shortcomings so that they feel free and safe to recognize their own.

8. ALLOW THEM TO SAFELY FAIL

We all learn from our mistakes, so allow your kid to make mistakes (within bounds that they do not harm themselves or anyone else mentally, physically or emotionally). This also builds resilience.

9. ACTIVELY LISTEN

Let them talk first and listen with your body language. Frequently say "tell me more" and never, if you can help it, say "at least." "At least" is typically dismissive.

10. GIVE THEM RESPONSIBILITY

It is better to give your kid responsibility now and teach them how to handle that responsibility while they are under your supervision, guidance and leadership. When they are adults, they will have had practice making good decisions and creating better habits.

11. PAY ATTENTION TO THEM

Invest your time, because even when they act like they don't care, they really do. Any positive (particularly, non-judgmental) time and energy you put into trying to better understand their world will be appreciated. It will show them that you are growing too!

12. ASSUME THE BEST

Your kid is developing opinions, philosophies, and ideas. Support them in their quest and don't assume they are being "smart" or rude. Use their remarks as conversation starters.

13. POSITIVELY GOSSIP

If you see your kid do something selfless, caring, or wise, recognize it and call them on it, privately or in front of others. Or you can even "positively gossip" about them behind their back by bragging on them to others. Trust us, it will come back around to them.

14. REMEMBER THE LITTLE THINGS

If you know they had a big test that day, ask them how it went or send them a text during the day letting them know you are thinking about them. If you know they are fighting with a friend, let them know you are praying and ask if there is anything you can do. Remember Posture

12 if you get a smug remark.

15. EXPLAIN YOUR DISCIPLINE

Instead of being enraged by their mistake, explain your discipline in a diplomatic way. No one is perfect, but actions have consequences. Once they have made it right, let it go—don't hold it over their head. They need to know that you will always be fair. Also make sure your discipline has a finish line.

16. REMEMBER NOT TO TAKE LIFE TOO SERIOUSLY

Engage with them in activities that bring joy to both of you and others. Consider even having a small fund just for things that bring you joy! Not everything has to be serious.

17. BE WILLING TO DO WHAT YOU ASK THEM TO DO

If you say no phones at the dinner table, all phones, including yours, should be in the other room.

18. BE EMPATHETIC

Don't always try to fix the problem, but instead consider telling your kid about a similar situation in your life. Be vulnerable and genuine.

19. ENGAGE IN THEIR INTERESTS

Do they like Snapchat? Get an account and learn how to use it. Regardless of whether you think it's interesting or not, they will appreciate the effort if you are curious and humble.

20. (THE REAL #1) PRAY FOR YOUR KID

The most important, yet easily forgotten Parenting Posture: a posture of prayer. Your kid belongs to God and is entrusted to you.

Which three will you focus on? Pondering this is worth every minute you can give it. Get off to a strong start and prepare to invest in the days to come. You won't regret it. We're thrilled to dive into this with you!

“

Warning!

You'll be tempted to implement what you learn immediately, but we'll encourage you to wait until Step Four before you grab your kid's phone and change all the settings!

”

4. The Key to Shaping Your Kid's Identity

This is a huge set-up for your *Smartphone Sanity* experience. Serving as a final capstone for each step, there are **four activities designed for you to have a positive experience** by connecting as a family around the smartphone conversation. The goal of these times is for you to come together, enjoy one another, and enter into conversation. This will set you up for success and for further conversations throughout the book and beyond. Regardless of your family's dynamic, we encourage you to jump in with both feet.

Every activity is built on the framework of three identity shaping concepts: **Experience, Story, & Blessing.**[3] Unleashing all three concepts are essential to redeem your family's story, especially in regard to smartphones. Here's an overview of each concept:

EXPERIENCE

An experience is any activity where you are rallied around a common purpose or goal which creates *purposeful proximity* with your kids. Professor of New Testament Theology, Kline Snodgrass says, "proximity produces impact." Every activity will help you craft a simple and meaningful experience to help you grow in your family smartphone experience.

STORY

Story is closely linked with experience because experiences build on each other to shape our story. Understanding your story reveals how

[3] Axis is deeply indebted to the ministry and friendship of Greg, Jesse, and Chris at Restoration Project, as they have heavily influenced our understanding of Experience, Story, and Blessing. Restoration Project is an amazing ministry for men to fully engage as fathers, husbands, and brothers. Check out restorationproject.net for more.

you came to be who you are now. Think about it—God is a storyteller. The Bible tells us the meta-narrative of *innocence* to *tragedy* to *struggle* to *restoration*. Many times, our own story follows these same themes and it shapes our identity. As parents we get to share our own story with our children and we get to be curious about their story. **Every activity will include a time to share some of your story and for you to be curious about others' stories.** Remember: vulnerability breeds vulnerability. If you are open and share about *innocence*, *tragedy*, *struggle*, and *restoration*, your kid will want to do the same.

BLESSING

Blessing, as a verb, does not refer to providing material provision, but instead it points out the image of God in someone. Blessing calls out and names a person's unique future inside of God's plan. *Let that idea soak into your mind for a moment!* Blessing is very different from mere encouragement.

Encouragement is situational whereas blessing is tied to someone's very identity. That's why every activity will be a chance for you to bless your child. This doesn't need to be heavy handed or forced . . . but it does have to be tied to their very being, as someone created in the image of God. So, be aware of their loves and talents and start to think about how they reflect the image of our good God. When you bless your kid, it consecrates their future, acknowledging that God has a beautiful path for them.

Who you are in the present (**experience**), who you've been in the past (**story**), who you're becoming in the future (**blessing**) are all woven together to shape our identity. During each activity you will leverage the framework of experience, story, and blessing to influence your children in ways that will shape their identity and set them apart for God. You will plan Activity 1 during the first step of *Smartphone Sanity*, and each subsequent activity during its corresponding step. Each activity is meant to enrich and solidify the content learned in that step. Think of it as a celebration of progress.

Additionally, most chapters end with an experience—a mini-activity to help you dig in to the material. We highly recommend these or we wouldn't have included them. However, life is busy. Do what you can, we ask nothing else.

GET PRAYER SUPPORT!

We at Axis believe smartphones are at the epicenter of a spiritual battle and we want your family to see your phones as something that can be used for good in God's Kingdom.

This book will help **you** think through all of the issues surrounding phones so that you are ready to help **your family** use their devices for the Glory of God. You shouldn't do this alone. Invite a close friend or family member to pray for you in this journey. This will be essential to remembering there is a spiritual battle going on for the lives of our kids, and that we can invite the authority of Jesus over everything related to smartphones in your home.

Email a close friend or family member who should be aware you're working through the issue of smartphones in your family. Tell them what you're doing and ask if they'll come alongside and pray for you and your family during this time. Consider asking them if they'd be willing to serve as a sounding board for you as you think these issues through for your family. Below is an email template you can use to email this person. Email them today if you can. Here are two templates:[4]

SHORTER TEMPLATE:

> I've invested in a book called *Smartphone Sanity*, an experience made by a Christian ministry called Axis to help me think through how I use my smartphone and particularly how to help my kid use their phone well.
>
> Will you pray for us in this experience and be available in case any of the lessons cause me to need to bounce ideas off of someone else?
>
> Thanks!
> *Your Signature*

---

[4] Prefer to copy and paste? Me too. Visit axis.org/sanity-email.

LONGER TEMPLATE:

I'm working through a book called *Smartphone Sanity* from a Christian ministry called Axis (axis.org) to explore how the smartphone impacts me and my kid. I'll be reading a handful of short chapters that consist of a lesson and an experience. Each of these readings will provide me with deeper thinking about how we can control the smartphones in our lives instead of letting our smartphones control us. This is especially important as we're in the tough phase of figuring this smartphone thing out.

I believe the smartphone is a very useful device, but so much evil can be accessed through this same technology. This is a way of life moving forward, and I simply want to help my kid learn how to use this device well while they're under my roof. That way when they become an adult and use a smartphone for the rest of their life, I'll know I did my best to train them to use it well.

As we enter into this series of lessons and experiences, would you be willing to support our family by praying for us? Also, would you be open to discussing any lessons that I need to process further with someone I trust?

Thanks!
Your Signature

“

***Blessing**, as a verb, does not refer to providing material provision, but instead it points out the image of God in someone. Blessing calls out and names a person's unique future inside of God's plan.*

”

STEP 1

refocus

refocus

5. Essential Conversation 1:
   Very Good, Cursed, & Redeemed.

6. New Map for Gen-Z

7. Fixed or Growth Mindset?

8. When Should I Buy My Kid a Phone?

9. Goal of Control or Freedom?

10. Success Stories! And Snapchat Case Study!

11. Activity 1: Yummy Desserts

5. Essential Conversation 1: Very Good, Cursed, & Redeemed.

Welcome to Step One: Refocus! In this section of *Smartphone Sanity* we uncover adjustments that must be made in how you and your family approach the smartphone "war." We will refocus our thinking about our smartphones by viewing them in light of God's story.

Thus, welcome to your first Essential Conversation! Each step starts off with an essential smartphone conversation rooted in Scripture. This sets the tone, giving strong scriptural roots to the technological conversation ahead. Here are Axis' Four Essential Smartphone Conversations:

Conversation 1:	**Very Good, Cursed, & Redeemed.**
Conversation 2:	What Is It For?
Conversation 3:	We are on a Journey of Trust with a Destination of Independence.
Conversation 4:	You Can Tell Me Anything!

Let's venture into Essential Conversation 1: Very Good, Cursed, and Redeemed by reading from Genesis and exploring the phrase "very good." Genesis 1 says,

> *So God created man in his own image,*
> *in the image of God he created him;*
> *male and female he created them.*
> *And God blessed them. And God said to them, "Be fruitful and multiply and fill the earth and subdue it, and have dominion over the fish of the sea and over the birds of the heavens and over every living thing that moves on the earth." And it was so. And God saw*

everything that he had made, and behold, it was very good.

— Genesis 1:27-28, 30b-31a

God makes humanity in His image and He puts us in charge of His very good world. This includes the raw materials that make the smartphone possible. So how could something that causes so much evil now be something that is part of God's "very good" world? *Well, simply put, we've forgotten our story.*

> *Start with wonder.*

So whenever you are frustrated with your kid's phone or other technology in your life, first try to find a way to appreciate and remember how phones can be very good. See if you can find a posture of wonder. Let yourself be in awe that God created the world very good. Think about the fact that God put humanity in charge as stewards of the world, and this frustrating bit of electronics is actually a grand expression of human culture, collaboration, and creativity.

Here are some ideas to get the juices flowing. According to a Business Insider article in December 2014, "smartphones have more computing power than all of NASA did when it started sending astronauts to the moon," over fifty years ago. Wow, has technology progressed! The article also shared this astounding fact: Smartphones also have more computing power than the computers sent up in NASA's spaceships today (apparently reliability is more important than computing power for NASA's purposes, but still our phones are quite powerful in light of that). What an incredible thought, that our phones are more powerful than the computers it took to get us to the moon!

Another astounding thing to consider is all the details it takes to make a single smartphone—materials from different regions being harnessed by designers, engineers, and production facilities transported to a store near you—that fits into your pocket. Truly incredible.[5] Seeing the complexity and collaboration needed to make such an amazing device leaves me with an incredible sense of wonder. However, the story doesn't end with "very good," as we all know. Next, let's talk about "cursed" by taking a look at Scripture:

> *The Lord God said to the serpent,*
> *". . . I will put enmity between you and the woman,*
> *and between your offspring and her offspring;*
> *he shall bruise your head,*
> *and you shall bruise his heel."*
> *And to Adam he said,*
> *". . . cursed is the ground because of you;*
> *in pain you shall eat of it all the days of your life;*
> *thorns and thistles it shall bring forth for you;*
> *and you shall eat the plants of the field.*
> *By the sweat of your face*
> *you shall eat bread,*
> *till you return to the ground,*
> *for out of it you were taken;*
> *for you are dust,*
> *and to dust you shall return."*
> *. . . the Lord God sent him out from the garden of Eden to work the ground from which he was taken.*
>
> — Genesis 3:14a, 15, 17a, 17c–19, 23b

So now this "very good" phone is also a part of the next chapter in God's story, which is the curse. The first thing to notice here is the incredible sense of loss that Adam and Eve endured when they were exiled from the garden. They lose their safe and peaceful dwelling place and they lose their close relationship with God. Adding insult to injury, everything is now under a curse and is caught in the tension of a spiritual war.

Thankfully that is not the whole story. Because of the life, death, and

[5] Check out axis.org/sanity-pencil for the coolest old school video about the economics and complexity of the pencil! If it takes that much to make a pencil, it must take an army to create the smartphone.

resurrection of Jesus, we get to the next step in the story . . . redemption. Jesus is taking our war-torn lives and world and reconciling them to their true purpose and place. Redemption takes relationships that are broken and makes them right. Again, let's go back to Scripture:

> *Therefore, if anyone is in Christ, he is a new creation. The old has passed away; behold, the new has come. All this is from God, who through Christ reconciled us to himself and gave us the ministry of reconciliation; that is, in Christ God was reconciling the world to himself, not counting their trespasses against them, and entrusting to us the message of reconciliation.*
>
> — 2 Corinthians 5:17-19

Lots of reconciling is happening in that scripture! The idea of reconciliation is all about right relationships; right relationships with God, with others, with ourselves, and with God's creation. Within all of those realms we have a ministry and message of reconciliation that reaches straight into our family and right to our phones.

In summary: we need to realize that our phones are very good and regard them with a sense of **wonder**. We must realize that there is a propensity for them to be cursed and misused therefore there is a sense of **loss**. And finally, we realize that because of Jesus we are redeemed and we have a ministry of reconciliation. We have a sense of **hope** that we can redeem our phones. The first Essential Conversation is, "How are our phones very good, how are they cursed, and how can we redeem them as a family?" Here is an ancient blessing as we journey forward:

> *The Lord bless you*
> *and keep you;*
> *the Lord make his face shine on you*
> *and be gracious to you;*
> *the Lord turn his face toward you*
> *and give you peace.*
>
> *— Numbers 6:24-26*

As you enter into Step One, and as you are thinking about the first

Essential Conversation, may you invite the Gospel into your home and may you submit your smartphone to God's story.

6. New Map for Gen-Z

We all know how distant we can feel from our son or daughter's phone experience. Sometimes, trying to enter their world is like stepping into a foreign country—you can't understand the language, you don't know the customs or faux pas, and you stick out like a jelly donut.

Wait. What? Yes, a jelly donut. Remember the time JFK was in West Berlin and tried to say he was a Berliner in German, but accidentally said he was a jelly donut?![6] Whoops! Thankfully his audience was gracious with him and appreciated the effort! Which is the same thing your kid will do for you as you work to understand their world if you have a posture of curiosity and appreciation.

After 13 years of speaking to hundreds of thousands of teens and parents, Axis has identified four key actions to being a good tourist in the foreign country of "Teen." We think of them like a map that helps us **Look, Know, Grow, and Talk.** These four disciplines need to be practiced on a regular basis in order to connect deeply with the heart of your kids. Miss one and the ability to connect with your kids is much more difficult. Do them all, and it's much easier.

LOOK

Look means to have **an awareness of the pop-culture, teen-culture, and technology trends in your kid's world.** It shows them you care about their language and culture. Unfortunately, these are constantly changing (weekly, it seems), and thus can be difficult to get a handle on. That's why we created our weekly Culture Translator email. We want to share our curated (and completely free) information with you,

[6] I don't care if it is true or not. It's funny, video at: axis.org/sanity-jelly. More politicians need to end their speeches self-identifying as pastries.

so sign up now at axis.org/ct![7] We hope you'll use it and find yourself more connected to the world of your kid as you look at their culture. This is especially important while working on your family's smartphone habits, since the smartphone is the main avenue your kid has to teen-culture.

KNOW

While **Look** is an awareness of what's going on, **Know is the ability to dig deeper and understand the details** of the pop-culture, teen-culture, and technology trends once you know they exist. To be able to fully define and understand teen trends on a regular basis is HUGE. How often have you thought, "I just don't understand!" Well, we want you to, and so does your kid! Throughout this book we will be providing a few opportunities to read our Parent Guides (for free) that detail the intricacies of various teen trends.

GROW

Grow has two sides to it. One is **finding sources of mentorship to help you grow as a parent.** The second is **growing in your own spiritual walk and developing your own habit formation**. If we're not growing as parents, then it's very difficult to expect our kid will desire to grow. Developing yourself ensures that you're healthy enough to lead your kid, and also provides a great example for them. At Axis we've interviewed over 250 parenting experts. We hope to impart much of their expertise in this book.

TALK

Talk, of course, is the ultimate goal in all of this. We want to see as many parents as possible **have One Lifelong Conversation with their children**. If you're not having a conversation with your kid about cultural, social, and theological issues, someone else is. That someone else could be your kid's peers, their friends' parents, or the mainstream culture via their phone.

---

7 This is easily one of Axis' best resources. It's pure parenting gold. After reading The Culture Translator your kids will be like, "Mom, how'd you know that, and how did you know how to pronounce it correctly?!?" Whatever you do, don't answer. Just nod slowly while smiling as smugly as possible.

The trick with Talk is that it's really hard to start here. A heart connection is needed for you to be able to have meaningful conversations with your kid. In most cases, to effectively start important conversations with your kid you must have learned to Look, Know, and Grow first. This isn't a guarantee, but it's highly likely. If you're able to have meaningful conversations with your kid about what's important to them and you, you've probably done something right. If this is difficult to do then you're normal, and it's never too late. You can start now. As you think about this chapter, think about how you can make Look, Know, Grow, and Talk more a part of your everyday thought process when it comes to your kid. Believe us, it will make all the difference.

EXPERIENCE: GO BUY YOURSELF A JELLY DONUT AND THEN PONDER DR. KARA POWELL

None of these actions are worth anything unless we are motivated by love. Dr. Kara Powell, professor, author, and Executive Director of Fuller Youth Institute, expounded on the importance of this in a video interview[8] she conducted with Axis about *warmth.* We'd like to share that with you, as we found it quite instructive.

Dr. Powell asked us, "Are you connected to your kid's heart?" What she meant was not their schedule, academics, or performance—*their heart*. How do you even do that? Most times this looks like connecting with your kid over what *they* are interested in. This will look different for each kid out there, as each kid has their own unique and beautiful interests.

Warmth, Dr Powell informed us, is not expecting them to step into your world, but rather learning to step into theirs, no matter how far it differs from your own interests. Maybe that's sitting down and watching a hockey game together. Or perhaps it's asking about their music or art. It could even be just sitting and listening to them talk

[8] Visit axis.org/sanity-drpowell to view this short and insightful interview. Dr. Powell's insight may have been the greatest leap I've had in my parenting journey in a few years. Want to keep reading and not watch the video? No problem. Read on, friend. We chose to include videos in this book because we like videos! Also, your kids like videos. Many of the videos will we share with you are worthy of being shared with your kids. It might even start a great conversation.

about their world.

We hope this encourages you to never miss an opportunity for warmth when **Looking, Knowing, Growing, and Talking** with your kid. Go buy yourself a jelly donut and think about how you can show warmth to your kid. You deserve it, and so do they.

7. Fixed or Growth Mindset?

We just discussed the importance of warmth, and ways you can **Look, Know, Grow, and Talk** to better enter your kid's world. Now let's look a little closer at **Grow.** What we will teach you about **Grow** will help you no longer be viewed as the "bad guy" in conflicts over your family's smartphones. As parents we realize that no parent is perfect, so it may take a long time to rebuild this bridge if a lot of damage has been done in this area.

Practice this: For every negative (or critical) thing you say or observe, try to say or observe four times as many positive things. No one likes to be around someone who always plays the role of the critic, and oftentimes that is where parents hover in regard to their kid's smartphone use. Trust me, I unfortunately know this all too well! If you always feel like the authoritarian "bad guy" when it comes to your kids phones, think on these two points:

1. Remember Very Good, Cursed, and Redeemed. Always invite the world in which we live into that narrative. Remember that it starts with wonder, shifts to loss, and ends with hope.
2. Don't be afraid to admire the beauty in something before critiquing whether or not it is true or good.

With these two shifts in mind, we hope that you can approach the smartphone conversation with a new mindset, not just when it comes to critiquing your kid, but in every way you parent. In fact, our hope is for you to model a Growth Mindset as you read this book. What do we mean? It means you are working to be a better parent today than you were yesterday, and you are eager to do the work to get there. You know the mistakes of your past are in the past. You are open, humble, and ready to become better today and the day after and the day after!

EXPERIENCE: LEARN AND REFLECT

You may have heard of Carol Dweck, author of *Mindset: The New Psychology of Success.*[9] Her book outlines what is called the Growth Mindset,[10] a seriously incredible concept for personal growth. Here's a quick summary for you:

> *There are two mindsets that have an immense effect on people's ability to learn: the fixed mindset, and the growth mindset. A fixed mindset is when someone believes that they are not in control of their abilities, that they cannot grow or learn, or that skills are something you are born with. A growth mindset is when someone believes that they are in control of their abilities, that they can grow or learn, and that skills are something you build over time.*
>
> *A fixed mindset tends to focus on performance, outcomes, or results, while a growth mindset focuses on the process of growing. Those with a fixed mindset tend to avoid the things that would help them grow the most, thus stunting their success both in the short and long run. Those with a growth mindset learn from and embrace challenges, allowing difficulties, challenges, and critiques to become opportunities for growth and success. This is a spectrum, and at different times you may fall into either category. But now that you can identify where you might fall on the spectrum at any given point, you can use that information to your advantage!*

Reflect on this knowledge to grow and learn by changing your mindset!

---

[9] You might prefer to watch a short video where we got this summary from as opposed to a book: axis.org/sanity-growth. Also, it is a great video to share with your kid.

[10] We went through a huge Growth Mindset phase at Axis (thank you to Chris!). Personally my wife and I went through a massive parenting and marriage shift because of the Growth Mindset concept too. It gives you the freedom to fail and the freedom to grow.

“

What do we mean by a Growth Mindset? It means you are working to be a better parent today than you were yesterday!

”

8. When Should I Buy My Kid a Phone?

You may be asking the question that every parent is asking: "When do I get my kid a phone?" or, "What if I already have given them a phone?" Axis gets asked this question *all the time*. The thing is, it's not as straightforward a question as you'd think. Actually, "When do I buy my kid a phone?" is the *wrong question*.

IT'S A TRAP![11]

This issue is deeper than a binary, either/or situation of your kid having a phone or not having one. Why? Because it matters less *when* you buy your kid a phone and it matters more *how* you allow them to use it. Asking "when" creates a false dichotomy, where your kid goes from not having a phone to having 100% access to a phone.

First, your kid will always have access to a phone (even if they don't own a phone) because of their friends. They won't have the same authority to customize it to their liking, but they will still have significant access. Second, getting a phone shouldn't necessarily mean they own it or have complete control over it. Possibly one of the biggest regrets we hear from parents is that they gave their kid a phone in the box it came in and set no use parameters. So, what's the answer? Glad you asked!

WE MUST REFOCUS THE QUESTION

When your kid has a phone, your goal must be to help them learn to use it responsibly, rather than letting them have it until they cross the line and then taking it away. One *essential* part of that process is making it very clear **you own the phone**, and your kid is being allowed to use it. Kind of like how you own your house and you allow your kid to use the

[11] Whatever you do, don't visit axis.org/sanity-trap . . . It's a trap.

room they call theirs. Notice that we have no language to easily describe this situation. Though your kid does not own the phone, we call it "their phone." No wonder many kids think the phone you bought for them to use is "theirs."

When you make it clear that *you* own the phone, then their claims to "privacy" fall flat. The phone is yours, and should be used as you see fit. They simply are allowed to use it under your supervision. This is the number one most important thing to emphasize when you give your kid a phone, or give it back to them. Be super clear about this. So, big picture-wise, we suggest giving your kid access to a phone you own with very limited functionality, and then over time (and through many discussions helping them develop wisdom), helping them learn to use it well before they leave your home.

There is so much to unpack here, hence the other chapters in *Smartphone Sanity*! But what you must understand is that this is not EITHER your kid has a phone with full freedom OR has no phone at all. **Instead this is a journey of growth with a destination of independence.**

Sometimes the hardest part is that this is not the norm. No matter what other parents are doing with their kids, stick to your guns! This will really matter for your kid's development into a mature and responsible adult.

NINJA PARENTS

One safety net a few clever parents made was to create a pact with other families in their circle about when they would all get their kids phones (and then when they would allow social media). They did this to avoid the frustration of hearing their kid complain about their friends having phones. That way this savvy mom could respond, "I know the Smiths' kids have them, but we don't and neither do the Jones, the Browns, or the Popielerczyks."[12] Strength in numbers!

OK, BUT WHAT IF MY KID ALREADY HAS A PHONE?!

Sure, you can just take their phone away from them forever and do a Hard Reset; but, that is not the purpose of this book. We recommend instead a "reboot." This assumes an intentional restart that properly

---

12 Everyone knows at least one family with a really interesting last name, right?

shuts down a system and then turns it back on in a healthy way. We will walk you through this. As a teaser, it will involve:

1. Asking forgiveness from them for giving them a phone without creating guidelines. (Yikes! You can do it!)
2. Telling them that you want them to have a phone and that you want to do it the right way.
3. Getting their feedback and making a plan **together**.

As we start learning to create limitations and guidelines for the "how" of your kid's phone use, remember that we are growing just as our kid is. Use your Growth Mindset. Be patient, kind, and warm!

EXPERIENCE: DOWNLOAD, THEN REFLECT

The first thing we'd like you to do is download and activate one of the following phone time-tracker apps. Scary, right!? They will come into play in a few chapters as we examine the allure of smartphones. For Android, there are lots of options! Try any of these: Space - Break Phone Addiction, QualityTime, My Addictometer, or Social Fever.[13] For the iPhone, there is no app necessary—just turn on Screen Time in Settings. *Inhale.* These apps do not share your information on phone usage. It stays between you, the app, and your phone. *Exhale.* After setting up an app, reflect on this quote from Stan and Brenna Jones, authors of the helpful series *God's Design for Sex*:

> *It's not enough just to set limits. We also need to help our children find other ways to get their needs met. The parent who sets limits but is not there to help and support the child is likely to be perceived by the child as cruel. We need to set the limits and provide the support.*

Reflect on what limits you place on your children. Do you also give them support when you do so? When did you feel this way about a limit your parents set for you? If you feel brave enough, consider sharing that story with your kid and tell them you've been trying to learn and grow as a parent.

---

[13] These apps need to stay running in the background to stay active. Shutting down the app fully deactivates it. Bleh.

“

Though your kid does not own their phone, we call it “their phone.”

9. Goal of Control or Freedom?

Congrats on finishing your first few chapters of *Smartphone Sanity!* That's a really big deal. Hopefully you've found a good groove![14] Right now, controlling your kid's phone might be the most important outcome of this book for you. We get that. Sometimes those phones can be infuriating. But today, we ask you to shift your goal from control (which you will get during Step Three of this book) to freedom (which will come much later, hopefully assisted by your investment of time and energy)!

Our goal is to help your kid learn how to use technology in a God-honoring way, one that will be their default even when they have no limits on them. Let us ask you something. What is freedom? Your kid might say: Doing whatever I want, whenever I want, however I want! Actually, most human beings might say just that . . . ***but is it true***?

THE JOURNEY OF FREEDOM

> *Seek freedom and become captive of your desires.*
> *Seek discipline and find your liberty.*
>
> — Frank Herbert, *Dune*

> *Therefore the good man, although he is a slave, is free; but the bad man, even if he reigns, is a slave, and that not of one man, but, what is far more grievous, of as many masters as he has vices.*
>
> — St. Augustine of Hippo, *City of God*

This feels self-apparent, but our kids are going to be adults—and it's going to happen more quickly than we'd like. Once they are adults they

[14] This dude has found his groove: axis.org/sanity-groove.

will be fully "free." So, they will get to decide how to spend their time and how to direct their wills. All parents *hope* that their children will make good choices . . . and we fear the alternative. The trouble is that children start out entirely governed by their parents. Infants are not free. They don't direct their actions at all. These two fixed points, full governance and full freedom, make up the parenting puzzle. So, how are we to help our kid make this transition?

The rubber meets the road when it comes to phones. Phones are the most powerful tool available to us right now. They multiply the number of actions that we can take dramatically, much more so than any other tool. This truth is much better put by one of my favorite Shower Thoughts:[15] If I tap my phone in the right places, a pizza will show up at my front door. This is striking because if you can get a pizza to appear by tapping your phone, what can't you do with it? The ocean of actions that become immediately available upon gaining a new phone could easily make up **the most significant gain in freedom that your kid will ever experience.**

> *If I tap my phone in the right places, a pizza will show up at my front door.*

And when people are given more freedom than they're ready for, they make bad choices. Imagine giving a three-year-old a bowl full of M&M's, and telling him, "Do whatever you want, but make a good decision . . ."

Ironically, although phones offer users a nearly unlimited range of opportunities—more opportunities than ever before in human history—a vast number of users (293 million monthly users and 2.73 billion downloads) spend those opportunities playing Candy Crush.

To escalate this insight, consider that the freedoms that parents

---

[15] Shout-out to my only brother, Daniel, who has his PhD in philosophy. This chapter is largely inspired by his thoughts.
Inspired = plagiarized. Thanks, Dr. Eaton ;)

ought to handle most carefully are those that have the highest stakes. Giving your kid the freedom to drive a car is something that comes late in the parenting game, because if the kid makes poor decisions while driving, then they could seriously injure or even kill themself or someone else. In many ways, phones are *more dangerous* than cars. When we think about the danger of cars we think about the violence that they might do to our bodies. Phones, however, can destroy our children's hearts and minds. And, according to Matthew chapter 5, that's *worse* than physical injury.

WHAT IS FREEDOM?

So what if freedom is NOT doing whatever, whenever, however? What if instead, it is having the ability to set wise boundaries for yourself that allowed you to flourish and not be enslaved? This is freedom *from* evil and the freedom to grow and mature. The freedom to do good.

PLAYING SOCCER, BY A CLIFF, WITHOUT A FENCE[16]

Surely the dangers that smartphones bring are frightening. Similarly, it would be terrifying to play soccer by a cliff without a fence. But if the appropriate boundary is in place, it almost disappears as you focus on enjoying the moment you are in, safe within the limits you have placed. The new goal here is not setting limits, but teaching your son or daughter to build fences on their own. This begins, as always, with making space for that conversation.

EXPERIENCE: WRITE A NOTE OR SEND A TEXT

We want you to **write a simple note to each of your kids**. This can be a **text message or a handwritten note** you put in their room or someplace they will find it. **Keep it short.** Tell them that you love them and that you are trying to grow and become a better parent. Part of that growth has to do with learning about smartphones and why they are amazing, and also how they have the potential to harm your family.

If appropriate ask them to pray for you in this journey and tell them

[16] I owe Randy, the Axis Board Chair, credit for this analogy. One of his many brilliant and well placed one-liners.

that you'll need their input and you want to learn from them along the way too. End by repeating you love them and by affirming something you admire about them. This will go a long way to opening up the conversation about smartphones, limitations, and freedom.

10. Success Stories! And Snapchat Case Study!

You are doing great! Hang in there and keep going.

This is a lighter chapter because we know how busy life can be, and we want to give you a little breathing room so you can stick with us. Remember, there are hundreds of other families who have read this book! Here are a few stories shared with us from parents after they read Step One about "being warm" with your kid. Be encouraged! After watching Dr. Powell's video on warmth, a mom said:

> *Instead of going to bed, because of course I'm tired, I called my son, and talked a while. Went upstairs to hang out with my daughter a few minutes. Just because. Just to be there. Baby steps. It's good.*
>
> Some more feedback:
> *We had thought we were deep past the point of no return with getting control of this issue and you are giving us so many helpful ideas. I feel so encouraged just knowing there are other families like us. We are not alone! Thank you again!*
>
> More thoughts from Dr. Powell's talk:
> *It was a convicting message as I am a very physically present parent that is often emotionally checked out. Or I am always looking at my kids more as workers than kids. I don't enjoy them like I want to, and I know I am not nearly as warm or affectionate as I need to be.*

You can do this, and you are not alone!

EXPERIENCE: READ THE CULTURE TRANSLATOR & READ THE PARENT'S GUIDE TO SNAPCHAT

Hopefully, you signed up for The Culture Translator,[17] and have this week's edition in your inbox. Read it and pay special attention to any trends regarding smartphones! Remember this is the discipline of **Looking**. Also, here are a few different Parent Guides on different forms of social media, each about 10 pages long. This is digging a little deeper, practicing the discipline of **Knowing**. We are including a free Parent's Guide to Snapchat for you to dive into. Or, you could choose to buy a different Parent Guide if your kids are into another platform. Our Parent Guides are just a few bucks.

Free Parent Guide Included with This Book:
Axis Parent's Guide to Snapchat[18]

Other Parent Guides for Sale at Axis.org/Guides:
Axis Parent's Guide to Instagram
Axis Parent's Guide to Tik Tok
Axis Parent's Guide to YouTube
Axis Parent's Guide to Fortnite
Axis Parent's Guide to Discord

---

[17] To sign up now, visit axis.org/ct.
[18] Just visit axis.org/sanity-snapchat. It's on the house!

11. Activity 1: Yummy Desserts!

This is a *meaningful* activity. Yet, we want you to feel no pressure, judgement, or shame as you think about doing your first activity. Our encouragement is to take one step at a time and embrace the opportunity to use this time as a chance to change the trajectory of your family. So, this is where you dig in with your kids around your smartphones. Understanding the impact of "experience"[19] is essential for this activity. The Romantic-Era poet, John Keats wrote in a letter on May 19, 1819:

> *Nothing ever becomes real till it is experienced—Even a Proverb is no proverb to you till your Life has illustrated it.*

> *Experience is at the forefront of the Gospel message.*

God shows us this in the Bible—it's full of stories of people learning through experience. It's not enough to know in your mind what communion is; receiving the elements is the transformational experience. In fact, the importance of experience is at the forefront of the Gospel message. God *came to us*, walked the earth *with us*, became human to be *among us*. It was (and is) experiential. Sure, information is important, but unless it enters into our life through experience, it can

[19] Axis is deeply indebted to the ministry Restoration Project for the design of these activities. We love their work: restorationproject.net.

never penetrate into our heart.

When we engage in experiences with each other, we not only allow for heart connection, but also subconsciously allow our hidden selves to emerge. As we get lost in whatever challenge we tackle together, who we really are shines forth for others to see. This is where the real growth happens. When we see these rays peek through, we can affirm each other's glory (the unique way we image God) and counter each other's shame (how our pain has convinced us we are inadequate).

That sounds great, but how do we accomplish such lofty goals as engaging with each other's glory and shame? Simply be aware. Notice what your kids say and what they *don't* say. When do they come alive or shut down? Activity 1 is about conversation, not interrogation! We hope you engage in the experience, and hopefully you are able to grow your heart connection with your kids.

EXPERIENCE: ACTIVITY 1!

Here are the details on how to set up your first activity with your kid. Before you do anything else, make sure you have at least one hour reserved and scheduled in the near future for the activity! Also each activity has three options. Do whichever you have time for![20]

1. Look, I'm Busy
2. You Can Do It!
3. The Overachiever Edition

WHAT'S THE ACTIVITY?

Experience: Eating your favorite desserts together.
Story: Sharing what you love about smartphones.
Blessing: Affirm something great about your kid's identity.

Here's How It Works: You will lead a family experience where you'll surprise your kids with an outing. The outing will be an intentional conversation about smartphones and will end with a grand finale—by surprising each of your kids with their favorite dessert. The goal of this time is to connect positively about the good parts of the smartphone.

---

[20] We wrote this to serve you! If these activities stress you out, skip them!

This is a great opportunity to show your kids that this can be a fun conversation and not something to be ashamed or nervous about discussing together. The dessert surprise is a great way to use this experience as an opportunity to show your love to your kids in a unique way and have some simple fun together.

OPTION 1: LOOK, I'M BUSY.

Step 1 and Done: Grab your kids' favorite ice cream at the store. Start a conversation about what you love about your phone. Ask them what they love about their phone. The End. A lot of ice cream shops[21] deliver via GrubHub or DoorDash if you want to make it even easier.

OPTION 2: YOU CAN DO IT!

Step 1: *Plan a 1-2 hour window in your calendar* and make sure all your kids can make it[22] (if possible).

Step 2: *Identify and reserve the location.* The goal here is simply to "break the script" and pick a setting that will make this memorable. This could be as simple as your back porch, a local park, or some other cool local spot. The idea is to pick a spot that is a little out of the ordinary for how your family normally operates so that they'll remember this for a long time. **Tip:** Pick a location that will work for the desserts you bring (it may need to be near a freezer or have a table to make serving dessert easy).

Step 3: *Pick a dessert your entire family loves.* You might need to do some recon to make sure you have something that works for everyone.

Step 4: *Commence experience and have a conversation about what you love about smartphones.* At the location, tell them you'd like to have a family conversation about smartphones. Tell them about your *Smartphone Sanity* experience (say however much or little you'd like), and that one of the experiences is to have a discussion with your kids about what they love about phones (this should work regardless of whether your kid currently has their own smartphone). **Tip: It's very important that this conversation has a positive tone,** so as to keep their defenses low and encourage them to be honest with their answers. A recommended

[21] Ever heard of Josh and John's Oatmeal Cookie ice cream? Game changer.
[22] Tip: Don't forget a kid ;)

opening question you can ask them is, "What are your top 4 favorite apps and why?" Parents should give their answers too. Be neutrally curious about their answers (don't come across as judging, critiquing, condemning). Be positive and have fun. Understanding, validating, and caring are keys to conversations like this.

Step 5: *Enjoy the dessert surprise!* The dessert reveal is your grand finale. You'll be tempted to lead with it. It'll be much more fun if you make it the surprise at the end of your time together. Make the location the appetizer, the conversation the main course, and the dessert, well, the dessert.

OPTION 3: OVERACHIEVER EDITION

I was once at a retreat where, a week before, they asked each attendee what their favorite dessert was. People answered truthfully, naming all the specifics of their favorite sweet treat. At the retreat after the speaker finished, they invited us into the kitchen, and voilá! Each of us easily spotted a single serving of our favorite dessert—down to each little detail—waiting for us! We felt so known and loved. This is the idea for the extended option. It's a perfect opportunity to love on your kid in a remarkable and impactful way.

Steps 1–2: Same instructions as Option 2.

Step 3: *Acquire dessert information.* It is never too late to ask your kid what their favorite dessert is! Make sure you get *exactly* what their favorite dessert is. The specifics matter! Try asking something like, "If you could only have dessert once more in your life, what exactly would you have?" Don't skimp on brand, extras, or particulars. This will certainly make it special and memorable. Additionally, get or create name cards for each kid. The purpose of the name card is to further individualize the experience, BUT also to create some curiosity. The dessert doesn't come out until the end of your time, so the cards are a simple way to create intrigue. The name card and dessert show personalization, but anything else you think of that personalizes for each kid will make it that much more special. Show them you know them and love them.

Step 4: Same instructions as Option 2. Additionally, do a smartphone stack at the beginning of your time by stacking your phones all in the center of the meeting area. Don't touch the phones while discussing. If someone does, they have to agree to do the do the dishes, or you can pick your favorite family chore for them to do. Agree verbally to the consequence ahead of time so as not to surprise the person who can't live without their phone (because that's a lot of us!). We hope these instructions help you on your way to a great activity together!

You've got this!

"

*We created these activities to **serve you!** If these activities **stress you out**, skip them!*

"

STEP 2

dangers

dangers

12. Essential Conversation 2: What Is It For?

Welcome to Step Two: Dangers! In this step we will discuss the dangers that smartphones present . . . both to you and your kid. Look forward to learning how to avoid some of the major pitfalls that can come from misusing smartphones. As you know, we start each step with an exploration of the scriptural foundation for one of Axis' Four Essential Smartphone Conversations. Now we look at Conversation 2.

Conversation 1:	Very Good, Cursed, & Redeemed.
Conversation 2:	**What Is It For?**
Conversation 3:	We are on a Journey of Trust with a Destination of Independence.
Conversation 4:	You Can Tell Me Anything!

The second Essential Conversation will prompt us to ask, "What is the smartphone for?" I love this question, because it reminds me to ask about the *telos*, the design or purpose, of the object in question. And really, Essential Conversation 2 is asking about *wisdom*. What are the wise decisions that need to be made about my family's smartphones?

To better understand the question "What is it for?," let's start by looking a little closer at the Hebrew word for wisdom: *hokhmah*. Marvin R. Wilson elaborates on the Hebrew understanding of *hokhmah* in his book, *Our Father Abraham: Jewish Roots of the Christian Faith*, an excerpt of which I've included below.

> *To the Greek, knowledge was the main way to virtue; the path to the good life was through the intellect. But to the Hebrew, wisdom went beyond intellectual pursuit; it was practical. Wisdom was established upon God-given principles of right and wrong. . . . Thus the Hebrews never viewed wisdom as mere factual*

> *information or as purely cognitive. Rather, it was skill in applying knowledge to a specific area. Wisdom began with the ability to see and evaluate all of life from God's point of view (Prov. 1:7). Wisdom had its seat in God . . . it usually implied the knack, know-how, or capacity to perform a particular task. Adroitness or cleverness might be called the handmaids of wisdom. . . . [The Bible talks about it as] leadership or administration (Gen. 41:33, 39; Deut. 34:9), the ability of a warrior (Prov. 21:22), the skill of a sailor (Ezek. 27:8), the technical know-how of garment making (Exod. 28:3), the cleverness to make artistic designs in gold, silver, and bronze (Exod. 31:3-5). In short, wisdom was the practical ability to function successfully, to the best possible advantage, in one's chosen area of service. Thus* hokhmah, *"wisdom," properly meant to have good sense, aptitude, or skill.*

We should think of three things when we think of *hokhmah*. First, *hokhmah* starts off grounded in the fear of the Lord. Second, because of the fear of the Lord, *hokhmah* is moral. Third, it doesn't end with just knowing moral distinctions, but *hokhmah* moves on to mean actually becoming good at something, gaining practical ability. So, applying that to the question, "What is my smartphone for," ask yourself if you are practicing all three facets of the meaning of *hokhmah*: Am I fearing God with my smartphone? Am I thinking about the morally right and wrong ways to use it? Then, am I becoming skilled at using it in the best way? Another way to understand wisdom in regard to the question, "What is it for?," comes from our friends at The Bible Project. The following excerpt comes from their video series on Wisdom Literature,

> *"What are the wise decisions that need to be made about my family's smartphones?"*

specifically the book of Proverbs.[23] In the excerpt below we see how Scripture personifies wisdom as a woman. Here's what she has to share:

> *So what makes Lady Wisdom so smart? Well, she can see things that most people don't see. She believes that there is an invisible creative force in the universe that can guide people in how they should live. And you can't see it—just like you can't see gravity—but it affects everything that we do.*
>
> *So what's this force? Well, in Hebrew it's called* hokhmah, *and it usually gets translated into English as "wisdom." It's an attribute of God that God used to create the world, and* hokhmah *has been woven into the fabric of things and how they work. So wherever people are making good, or just, or wise decisions, they're tapping into* hokhmah. *And wherever someone is making a bad decision, they're working against* hokhmah . . . *Or, as it says in Proverbs chapter one, "The waywardness of fools will destroy them, but the one who listens to wisdom lives in security."*
>
> *So, it's like a moral law of the universe . . . It's a cause-effect pattern, and no one can escape it. And Proverbs personifies all of this as a woman . . . Lady Wisdom . . . She roams around the earth, calling out, making herself available to anyone who's willing to listen to her and to learn. Which leads to the second thing Proverbs believes: that anyone can access and interact with wisdom, and use it to make a beautiful life for yourself or for others. You can create with it like a designer . . .*
>
> *In fact,* hokhmah *in Hebrew isn't simply intellectual knowledge. The word is also used to describe a skilled artisan who excels at their craft, like woodworking or stonemasonry. So you show you possess* hokhmah *when you put it to work, and develop the skill of making a good life.*

What a refreshing way to explain the Hebrew concept of wisdom! Hopefully that will cement the concept of *hokhmah* for you as you ask yourself what the smartphone is for, and as you delve into the dangers

[23] Watch the video at axis.org/sanity-wisdom. It's definitely worth sharing this video with your kid. The Bible Project is the best.

it poses to you and your family. Let's go to James for a few final thoughts on wisdom:

> *Who is wise and understanding among you? By his good conduct let him show his works in the meekness of wisdom. But if you have bitter jealousy and selfish ambition in your hearts, do not boast and be false to the truth. This is not the wisdom that comes down from above, but is earthly, unspiritual, demonic. For where jealousy and selfish ambition exist, there will be disorder and every vile practice. But the wisdom from above is first pure, then peaceable, gentle, open to reason, full of mercy and good fruits, impartial and sincere. And a harvest of righteousness is sown in peace by those who make peace.*
>
> — James 3:13-18

Again, the idea of "What is it for?" is about wisdom. Biblical wisdom. *Hokhmah* is based in the fear of the Lord, driven by a knowledge of moral right and wrong, and blessed by good fruits. It's practical, it's functional, it works! We'll leave you with a final thought—who was the wisest person to ever live? Typically we would say Solomon; however, in Luke 11 it says, "The queen of the South will rise up at the judgment with the men of this generation and condemn them, for she came from the ends of the earth to hear the wisdom of Solomon, *and behold, something greater than Solomon is here*" (verse 31). This is referring to Jesus, saying that Jesus is the wisest. As the incarnation of God, Jesus is the wisest person to ever live. He will give you wisdom as you wade through asking what the smartphone is for. I will leave you again with this ancient blessing as we go into Step Two seeking wisdom:

> *The Lord bless you*
> *and keep you;*
> *the Lord make his face shine on you*
> *and be gracious to you;*
> *the Lord turn his face toward you*
> *and give you peace.*
>
> — Numbers 6:24-26

As you begin Step Two, may you pursue wisdom and truly understand what the smartphone is for.

Our devices are designed to keep us "hooked," with layer upon layer of social engineering baked in.

13. 2,600 Taps, Swipes, & Touches

It's easy to cast blame on our kids for their phone use, but what about us? Are we less addicted? Often, I feel uncomfortable knowing that my smartphone is the first thing I touch when I wake up in the morning and the last thing I touch before I go to sleep at night. *So how many times do we touch our phones each day?*

According to a study conducted by dscout, a human insight research company, the *average* smartphone user touches their phone 2,600+ times every day. What about extreme smartphone users? The top 10% touch their phones more than 5,400 times daily. A touch includes any time you swipe, tap, or type, and it is not the same thing as picking up your phone—which is a whole different issue altogether. You might not believe how many times you pick up your phone every day!

If there is one video you need watch from this book, preferably with your kid, it is episode one of the series "By Design," on the Vox YouTube channel.[24] It guest-stars Tristan Harris, co-founder of the Center for Humane Technology, a non-profit dedicated to "Reversing the digital attention crisis and realigning technology with humanity's best interests." Tristan Harris used to be Google's Design Ethicist, so he knows the ins-and-outs of how technology harnesses users' attention, and how lucrative that attention can be for tech companies. After realizing how apps and technologies compete for the user's attention—ultimately to the detriment of the user—he left Google to advocate for "humane technology," technology that respects and protects the user's welfare over the tech company's. Since then he has called-out ways technology draws us to serve it, rather than it serving us.

---

[24] Seriously. If you watch any video in this book it needs to be this one: axis.org/sanity-addiction. If you share or text any video in this book to your kid, again, it should be this one. Can't beat that line about "2 Billion Truman Shows."

The video that Vox created about Harris explains these addictive qualities built-in to today's technology very clearly. Our devices are *designed* to keep us "hooked," with layer upon layer of social engineering baked in. Take notifications, for example. In the case of a call, text, or message, another person wants to communicate with you. This is a true social interaction. Many apps, however, mimic this stimulus to get you to spend more time on their platform. They feed off our natural desire for relationships by sending push notifications about posts, comments, likes, and interests that only vaguely involve you or the connected person. This usually leaves us feeling unfulfilled.

But sometimes, there is that one comment directly responding to you, or perhaps a direct message, mixed in with the grab-bag of other notifications. This randomness, with real social interaction thrown in the mix, is addicting. Tristan explains that if this mix of notifications was predictably bad or predictably good, then we would not get addicted. The random nature is what hooks us.

This is the same social engineering behind slot-machines. Vox claims that slot-machines make more money (in the US) than baseball, movies, and theme parks *combined*, and that slot-machines become addictive about 3-4 times faster than other types of gambling. Many apps even mimic pulling a slot-machine lever with the "pull to refresh" function. They could continually update the feed, but they instead designed this little lever for us to pull. Feel like a rat in a lab yet?[25]

Another way phones keep us engaged is by the manipulation of our eye patterns through color. Our eyes are attracted to warm or bright colors, bright red being at the top of that list. Think: notification bubbles. App icons also tend to be designed or redesigned with bright, bold colors. Harris compares this, again, to slot machines. They have bright colors, fast movement, flashing lights, and sounds to accompany pulling the lever. All of these inputs are a subconscious pull on our attention. Their sensory experience, or siren's song, are designed into the pixels of Instagram.

One last trick apps use that is explained in Vox's video is what Harris aptly calls "bottomless vortexes of stuff." What he means by this is infinite scrolling and auto-play. This never ending stream of data is

---

[25] No joke. Type "B.F. Skinner, variable ratio reinforcement" into Google. It's the behavioral science behind slot machines. Fascinating!

what the band Arcade Fire parodies in the lyric, "Infinite content, infinite content, infinitely content?"

In contrast to pagination, infinite scrolling and auto-play have no built-in endpoint. Users do not click "next" to progress to more material; it is just loaded for them. This greatly decreases our control over the amount of content consumed, as our brains rely heavily on visual cues (as opposed to our own sense of satisfaction) to stop consumption. That's why it's so easy to blow forty minutes on Insta like it's nothing.[26] Harris ends the video with the difficult question, "What is genuinely worth your attention?" We hope you ponder this during this chapter's experience.

EXPERIENCE: TIME FOR A LITTLE SELF-INSPECTION

Time to become your own lab experiment! We have some fun challenges for you to take. Take them all or just pick one . . . and feel free to invite a friend to do it with you. The goal of these is to become more self-aware, have fun, and lead by example. You can do it!

A few chapters ago we asked you to download and/or activate a time-tracking app for your phone. There are many features of these apps but the one thing we want you to report on is this: How many times do you pick-up your phone in a day, and when? Does it feel like a lot or a little? Any interesting patterns? There are many triggers influencing how you interact with your phone. Pick one or all of these challenges and see how they impact your phone use.

1. ***Notifications.*** Take a few minutes and review all of your notifications. Remove all non-human notifications.
2. ***Delete It!*** Consider deleting "that" app from your phone for a week. You know the one we are talking about. It's the one that is taking up all your spare moments of boredom. For me it is email.[27] For you it could be Facebook or Insta. Or Candy Crush. I mean, it *is* really

[26] Or watch three episodes of *Stranger Things* in a row instead of just one. Thanks autoplay.

[27] I know. I'm that exciting. I literally don't have an email app on my phone unless I am traveling. My latest #GrowthMindset experiment is leaving my phone in my car when I get home from work a few times a week. It's hard to do!

addicting . . . And don't forget Clash of Clans. Somehow it is "Free-to-Play," yet it has made +$6B!

3. ***Grayscale.*** In the accessibility settings, turn off color and only use grayscale. This removes some of the fun from looking at your screen.
4. ***Autoplay.*** Do you have Netflix[28] or YouTube on your phone, TV, or computer? In the settings turn off autoplay. We dare you.
5. ***Clean-up your Home(screen).*** Put only the essential tools for everyday-life on the home-screen of your phone. Keep entertainment and "bottomless vortexes of stuff" tucked away and out of sight. Yes, this includes anything with infinite scrolling.[29]

Remember. It is not what you are running from . . . it is what you are running to. In this situation, you are running toward more human connection and creative actions. We are using wisdom to use our phones how *we* want to, not giving in to how *they* try to control *us*.

Lastly, we want you to think on this: How does looking at your own smartphone behavior make you consider how you may lead your own kid with their phone? Your next activity will have you confess something about your own smartphone misuse with your kid. Start thinking about your answer now.

[28] *We compete with sleep and we're winning.* Reed Hastings, Netflix CEO

[29] I can't stop hearing the grating chorus of Arcade Fire's *Everything Now*: "Infinite content! Infinite content! Infinitely content?"

14. Screen Addiction

We all get 24 hours in a day. So, how many of those 24 hours do we spend with our phones? Considering that we are probably asleep for 8 of those hours, we're really looking at an average of 16 hours of potential screen time. Here's what one study from Common Sense Media found for screen time of different ages:

- 6 hours per day for 8 to 12 year olds
- 9 hours per day for teens
- 9 hours per day for adults

And the real surprise? Most people assume they spend half as much time on their phone than they actually do. What's your result? Likely a surprising number! So why do we spend so much time on our phones. One answer is dopamine.[30]

1. DOPAMINE: A HAPPY, ADDICTIVE CHEMICAL

Every single time you receive a notification on your phone, your brain releases dopamine. This is the same chemical that is released during sex and gambling (as well as a key component to cocaine and heroin addiction!). If we touch our phone 2,600 times a day, we get 2,600 small hits of dopamine.

2. THE SOUND OF ANXIETY

In a study covered on 60 minutes entitled "Brain Hacking," Guy Campanile and Andrew Bast uncover ways that smartphones lure us in and punish us for not picking them up. Anderson Cooper participates as

30 We're not exaggerating about any of this research. View the studies at axis.org/sanity-dope.

the subject to prove that we experience anxiety when we do not immediately check our phones when we hear or see a notification. Furthermore, this anxiety occurs because your brain wants to receive the dopamine that comes from seeing and interacting with that notification.

3. SMARTPHONE: SURVIVAL INSTINCT?

Dopamine is released following tactics intrinsic to our survival including: reproduction, eating a delicious meal, exercising, and hunting. When you are on your phone, you are typically "hunting" for something, such as entertainment, social interaction, a product, or information on a subject. The process of hunting alone releases dopamine and thereby makes you feel as though you are accomplishing something important. Not only is dopamine released during typical primal processes such as hunting and eating, it is also released following a SUCCESSFUL social interaction. Your Instagram has, in short, fulfilled the requirements in your brain of being an important successful member of society.

4. BIOLOGY

While our brains do all sorts of unbelievable things, they have four very specific "pathways" or neurotransmitters that are highly affected by dopamine. Three out of the four pathways (the mesocortical, mesolimbic, nigrostriatal) are commonly referred to as the "reward pathways." When someone is addicted to dopamine, these begin to work incorrectly. Think of these pathways like a beaten path. The first time someone walks down a path, you may not even see a footprint. However, over time as you walk down the same path, say 2,600 times per day, you begin to see a clear and strong path that is hard to ignore and nearly impossible to return to its original footprint-less state. This process is called "long term potentiation." The once, "road less traveled by" can quickly turn into a fully paved highway.

5. YOU MAY HAVE A GAMBLING PROBLEM

As we mentioned before, smartphone addicts have a great deal in common with those addicted to gambling. The concept of "Variable Reward Schedules" was introduced in the 1930s by psychologist B.F

Skinner through his experiment with mice. The basic concept is that mice (and humans!) respond to reward associated stimuli (such as smartphones) when the reward is distributed randomly or at varying times. The mice would interact with given stimuli more often when they were not sure which times they would receive a reward. As mentioned before, this is where the parallels between our instinct to hunt and our attraction to smartphones are drawn. Gambling: enter a quarter, pull a lever, and win or lose. Smartphone: open the app, pull down to refresh, and you will find something interesting or you won't.

6. HABITS

Habits are hard to form, or are they? A so-called "streak" is a powerful tool for creating habits. Being on a diet and not wanting to "break your streak" by eating sweets helps form the habit of eating healthier food. "Snapstreaks" work the exact same way, keeping you Snapchatting long into the night. In the same way that the possibility for reward causes us to pull the lever at a casino, the possibility of having someone send us a photo on Snapchat is enough for us to check it. Pretty soon you keep your phone open to Snapchat out of convenience . . . and habit.

7. IT'S NOT JUST YOU

Instagram algorithms[31] often withhold "likes". . . then they submit them all at once so we receive a stronger burst of dopamine. You are one of millions of guinea pigs in their experiment to find the most engaging user experience. In the words of Tristan Harris, they are actually "brain hacking" you and millions of users to get you to come back again and again.

8. SEEK AND YE SHALL CONTINUE SEEKING . . .

Dopamine pairs well with opioids in delivering pleasure. The search for dopamine release is similar to our hunting instinct, like we mentioned in number three. A study done on rats showed that when the neurotransmitters we mentioned earlier are destroyed, rats will starve to death even when their food is within reach. They simply lost the desire to find the food. Interestingly, an article from *Psychology Today*

[31] Another great video worth watching with your awesome kid. Instagram will never be the same. See axis.org/sanity-hacked to get the scoop on how you're being brain-hacked!

claims our dopamine cravings have the potential to never be satisfied. We could continue scrolling through Facebook for hours without blinking an eye.

9. VERY GOOD AND CURSED

As we have said before, all technology—as with all of God's creation—is very good, but falls under the curse just like everything else. Referring back to the power of streaks, some app creators are using the same neurological information that Instagram and Snapchat use to create positive habits. Apps like the YouVersion Bible app uses streaks to help you stay on track with reading your Bible every day. It also sends you notifications like Facebook and Instagram when someone likes a verse image you created or a passage you underlined. That positive reinforcement releases dopamine in the same way that any other app would, but helps you form a positive habit.

THE JURY IS IN

Clearly phones are scientifically addictive. Johann Hari has an excellent TED talk[32] on the subject, which we will briefly summarize for you here:

> *Disconnection is a key driver of addiction. We might think we live in the most connected world yet, but these messages and media are just a parody of human connection. In the case of a crisis, it won't be your Twitter followers that come to sit with you but rather your deep, face-to-face relationships that help you turn it around. In fact, the number of close friends that the average American believes they could call on in a crisis has been steadily declining since 1950. As a culture, we're one of the loneliest societies*

> *The opposite of addiction is not sobriety but connection.*
>
> ~Johann Hari

[32] Another life changing video: axis.org/sanity-connection.

that has ever been. This kind of distance fuels addiction, even addiction to your smartphone. But the good news is that the opposite of addiction is not sobriety, but connection. Pursue a heart connection with the addicts in your life, telling them you love them and care for them—regardless of their actions.

As Johann Hari implied, **the path to you and your kid's ability to use phones without addiction is to better connect with one another.** Real connection is the antidote to how the smartphone tries to addict us. Creating space for that connection is what our next experience is all about.

EXPERIENCE: TUCK YOUR PHONE INTO BED . . .

. . . in the kitchen.[33] Here's how. Get online and order an old school alarm clock or just swing by the closest big box store and buy one. The cheapest ones we found were a whopping $4. Use that alarm clock instead of the alarm on your phone. Since you don't need your phone alarm you can store it away from you in the kitchen at night. Creating this simple boundary is a giant step toward more sleep and toward defining sacred space where the phone is not running your life.

Remember this is just an experiment! Trying new things like this shows you have a Growth Mindset and are eager to try new ways of improving as a person. A pleasant side effect of this is that you will create curiosity with your kids. They will want to know why Mom and Dad are trying so many weird new things . . . and they may even want to join you.

33 Or, I triple dog dare you to leave your phone in your car a few days a week (starting at 5p and then leaving it there overnight) . . . And yes, I just referenced the greatest Christmas movie of all time. Merry Christmas. Want to watch the clip? axis.org/sanity-tripledogdareyou

15. The "S" Word

Now we're going to take what may feel like a strange turn. We've been talking about the physical and habitual dangers of our phones. But now we're going to address a major obstacle to discussing all of these issues as families. That obstacle is the "S" word. That's right, you know what we mean, the relationship killer known as . . . *shame*. **As we enter into the world of shame we're going to need you to be BRAVE.** Nobody speaks about shame better than Dr. Brené Brown. Here is what she has to teach us about shame:[34]

> *There is a huge difference between guilt and shame. Guilt is a focus on behavior, while shame is a focus on self. Guilt says, "I did something bad," while shame says, "I am bad." Shame is highly correlated with addiction, depression, violence, aggression, bullying, suicide, eating disorders, etc. Guilt, on the other hand, is inversely correlated with those same issues. Shame is an epidemic in our culture; and, to find our way back to each other, we have to understand how it affects us and those around us. To do this, we must have empathy for each other, as empathy is the antidote to shame. Shame grows if it is surrounded by secrecy, silence, and judgement. If met with empathy, shame dies. That's why the most powerful words to hear when feeling ashamed are, "Me, too." If we are truly going to find our way to each other's hearts, vulnerability and empathy are the path.*

Sounds simple, but it is really hard to engage shame with empathy and vulnerability. Therefore, we have some more guidance from Dr. Dan

[34] Dr. Brown is known as a bestselling author, cutting edge researcher, and thrilling storyteller. Catch her TED Talk on shame at axis.org/sanity-shame to enjoy all three of her skills at once.

Allender,[35] a prominent Christian author, professor, and therapist, from a video interview he participated in with Axis.[36] He says that to deal with the topic of shame you have to talk about your own experiences with it. This means that we as parents must bring our shame to the conversation in order to offer a model of how to engage with it in a healthy way. Dr. Allender keenly states that shame isn't what God desires for us; there is no "good" shame. Shame, fundamentally, is us turning against our own heart. Think about it . . . What does a child do when they get caught doing something bad? They cover their face, trying to hide from shame. What did Adam and Eve do in the Garden after they disobeyed? They covered themselves with leaves.

If you name Shame and talk about it—creating a collaborative conversation with your kids—you can foster learning and healing. One way to cultivate a space for this healing is to create what Dr. Allender calls a "No-contempt Zone" in your home. Contempt is the belief that a person or thing is beneath consideration, worthless, or deserving of scorn. Contempt compounds shame in a similar way to Dr. Brown's three shame catalysts of secrecy, silence, and judgement. Not only that, but contempt stunts any chance for resolutions to be made. There will be no healing, learning, or growing if there is a feeling of contempt lingering. It's a form of isolation, keeping us from connecting!

By owning up to and talking about your own shame to your kids, you show them the way to battle shame, and that they can bring their shame to the table without fear of judgement. It may not be easy, but it's worth it. It's likely you're very uncomfortable right now. As Dr. Allender says, "Shame has a transmittable and contagious effect." What this means is that when someone else discusses shame, it is likely to cause the reader's shame to come to the surface in their own mind.[37]

EXPERIENCE: ASK YOURSELF, ASK YOUR KIDS

From now on, practice confession and vulnerability with your teens, and use your smartphone as the training ground. Ask yourself these

[35] I got the flu thanks to someone bringing their sick kid to my gym's childcare and thus infecting my whole family. I'm not bitter. While I was sick I went through an entire online course by Dr. Allender. His insights into the human condition are mind bending.

[36] Dr. Allender explains shame, the "No-contempt Zone," and much more in his interview with Axis. You can find it at axis.org/sanity-shame.

[37] Like we are doing right now. Sorry.

questions, informed by Dr. Brown & Dr. Allender:

1. Do I feel guilty about any aspect of my phone usage? If so, how?
2. Do I carry any shame regarding my phone usage? If so, can I pinpoint that shame?
3. What can I do today to make my home a "No-contempt Zone?"

During an upcoming dinner or car ride tell your kids how you learned about the difference between shame and guilt. Define the difference for your kids and see what conversation ensues. Here are some easy definitions to remember and bolster the conversation:

Guilt (as defined by Dr. Brown): A focus on behavior. I did something bad. "I'm sorry, I made a mistake."

Shame (as defined by Dr. Brown): A focus on self. I am bad. "I'm sorry, I am a mistake."

Contempt (as defined by Dr. Allender): The feeling that a person or thing is beneath consideration, worthless, or deserving scorn.

> *Shame grows if it is surrounded by secrecy, silence, and judgement. If met with empathy, shame dies. Empathy is the antidote to shame.*
>
> ~Dr. Brené Brown

16. Five Pathologies

We understand the last two chapters have been quite heavy and this chapter will not be lighter. It won't take much mental work to read, but it is heavy because of the weight of the issues we'll be addressing. Please hang in there. Your kid's body and soul are at stake and you need to know what they are up against.

Remember, Steps Three and Four of *Smartphone Sanity* will raise your spirits with hope and provide strategies that will protect your family. Chances are that the issues we'll address are some of the reasons you picked up this book in the first place. Time to get re-motivated and calibrated for the final two steps where things will get a lot more practical.

THE 5 SMARTPHONE PATHOLOGIES

As parents, we're well aware that there are a lot of bad things our kid could run into on their phone. This is traditionally the number one concern parents have when considering whether or not to let their kid have a phone. Now we'll be exploring 5 Smartphone Pathologies that we've identified.[38] This isn't intended to overwhelm (. . . but it will). It's intended to inform and contextualize so that we can start working on how to address these issues in Step Three. The first two pathologies are passive in nature while the last three are active. We think you'll see what we mean.

One recommendation we have for this moment: Consider pausing and praying for wisdom and peace as you read about these items. Let God cover you and your kids as you reflect on these difficult issues.

[38] If you'd like to dig deeper, all articles and studies that fueled this chapter can be found at axis.org/sanity-danger.

ONE: PASSIVE IGNORANCE

These are factors of smartphone use which are primarily physical in nature that the smartphone user may be ignorant of until they learn the truth.

Eyes: Various studies have looked at the effect of smartphones on our eyes. Recent findings show that looking at screens won't harm your physical eye, BUT could cause harm to your visual system. However, some studies say screen time can damage young eyes with problems like myopia.

Brain: You can take the rabbit hole pretty deep on studies people have done on the brain. Whether it's brain imbalances or brain jitteriness, more and more folks are starting to document the effects smartphones have on our brains. Children and teens are especially at risk. We should continue to pay attention to this.

Thumbs & Necks: Tendons (in thumbs, etc.) and necks can also be at risk with extended smartphone use.

Carcinogens: Some think that radiation or electromagnetic fields are what we should be really concerned about, including the World Health Organization.

Habits: We talked about this in detail in the chapter on touches, taps, and swipes, but our habits are impacted by smartphones intentionally. They want us to be addicted to them. Each app is jealous for our time so they work hard to out-manipulate one another.

Sleep: Smartphone use can negatively affect our sleep, and possibly more when you use it at night. Sleeping with your phone also means you're never away from it.

TWO: PASSIVE INNOCENCE

These are factors of smartphone use which innocent kids with smartphones might stumble upon unintentionally the first time. As one mom said, "My twins weren't looking for the darkness, but the darkness was looking for them."[39]

Bullying: Cyberbullying can take on a lot of different forms. It can be more in-your-face, like traditional in-person bullying; or, it can take

---

[39] Referring to a high-school upperclassmen asking one of her junior-high daughters for nudes . . . via a series of text messages.

on a more passive approach, like online gossip. Smartphones, when in the hands of a bully or a gossiper, can cause significant harm to any innocent victim, whether they have a smartphone or not.

Predators: As a recent article from Independent.ie says, "Pedophiles used to pretend they had a vocation so they could get at children, while others became experts in the sport of their choice to obtain access to them; these days pedophiles become incredibly knowledgeable and skilled at using apps like Musical.ly [now named TikTok], Instagram or certain Xbox games, just so they can impress their prey." It's a new world with online predators. They can target innocent kids and teens through apps and games and with great success. "Catfishing" and online scams can also really surprise an innocent kid and ruin their day, year, or life.

Dangerous Ideas: Music apps, online video platforms, news articles, and blogs can open up your kid to new ideas by unknown sources without supervision. Simple access to so many facts and opinions can cause innocent kids to be influenced with dangerous ideas from the wrong places. Without the encouragement of dialogue and a biblical worldview as a lens, intellectual innocence can be lost without parents having a clue. As you may have seen a couple of chapters ago, we talk about many of these ideas as they surface weekly in the free Axis Culture Translator email.

Porn: The average age of first porn exposure seems to be dropping as younger kids get access to smartphones. It's just one accidental click away. Tony Perkins has some particularly insightful things to say on this on the Family Research Council website. We highly recommend his writings speaking out against the proliferation of pornography in our culture.

Sexting: More and more teens are sexting. ABC News recently reported that almost 27% of teens are receiving sexts, and about 15% are sending them. Once a sext is out there it can be shared with your kid whether they ask for it or not and without the consent of the person of whom the picture was taken. All the person who wants to send the sext needs is your kid's number.

THREE: ACTIVE PARTICIPATION

When one is a participant, they accept and continue (although potentially reluctantly) to engage in continual unhealthy smartphone behavior like:

- Over-use
- Pornography
- Sexting
- Participating in Online Gossip
- Online Pranking
- Video Binging
- Participating in Secret Groups or Affinity Groups
- Secret Communication with Peers
- Hiding Activity
- Sneaking After-Hours Use
- Excessive Gaming

FOUR: ACTIVE BELLIGERENCE

When one is belligerent they begin intentionally influencing others' behavior in negative ways. In addition to the participant list, here's where one who is belligerent may go further:

- Introducing Others to Porn
- Sending or Requesting Sexts
- Being the Bully or Gossiper
- Using Secret Apps
- Encouraging Others to Abuse Phones

FIVE: ACTIVELY DAMAGING

This is a worst-case-scenario pathology. This is truly what we want to avoid at all costs by helping our kid practice good smartphone use now so they can be healthy moving into adulthood. All parents need to be aware that there is a risk of a slippery slope in using smartphones. These are some of the ultimate dangers:

- Addiction
- Being Convinced to Experiment in Harmful Behavior to Self or Others
- Being Encouraged to Pursue Harmful Lifestyle Alternatives (Gender Dysphoria, Homosexuality, Sexual Promiscuity, Alcohol & Drug Use, Eating Disorders)

- Depression
- Self-Harm
- Suicidal Ideation and Suicide

Be encouraged that there is hope. and we're here to help you learn how to enter into your kid world wherever they are on the ignorant-innocent-participant-belligerent-damaged continuum.

EXPERIENCE: GUIDED PRAYER THROUGH SCRIPTURE

If you feel overwhelmed, know that you are not alone. Take a few moments and grab a paper Bible. Open up the Psalms and read a few as prayers to God. Consider Psalm 46 or Psalm 51.

At this point you may hate your phone. If you do, try to remember that it is a part of a bigger story, a bigger history. It is very good, cursed, and can be redeemed. An example of this is the Dwell App.[40] Download the app, create a login, and listen to a few Psalms.

[40] I personally pay for the premium version of Dwell. I love it. Bravo, Dwell App, bravo! Oh . . . and I love listening to Felix read. He's the best! Find them at DwellApp.io.

17. Success Stories! And Sexting Case Study!

There are only two more steps left! Great job, you are halfway there! **Don't forget there are hundreds of other families who have gone through this book.** People have shared stories from their experiences, and we'd love to share them ALL with you but, we will keep this one short:

> *The activity for Step One was fantastic. We had a blast getting the table all fancy and having the girls come in and sit at their name tag places. We put all smartphones, tablets, and computers in the middle of the table and talked for almost 2 hours about the "very good" aspects of the devices, our favorite apps and programs, and the things we really enjoy doing with technology. Then, we had delicious desserts. Finally, the girls taught us a new card game. It was a great time. Thank you so much for organizing all of this.*
>
> *This is so needed – more than anyone will probably admit – I love having a playbook on smartphones from a Christian worldview.*
>
> Smartphone Sanity *is going great! We feel it is growing everybody, we were so enlightened by the chapter on addiction. I feel like this has opened great conversation for all of us and we are making huge changes. This is helping us all be on the same page.*

EXPERIENCE: SKIM THE CULTURE TRANSLATOR & READ THE AXIS PARENT'S GUIDE TO SEXTING

Hopefully you have The Culture Translator in your inbox after signing up at axis.org/ct. Read it and pay special attention to any trends regarding student culture, especially technology! There is always something worthy of a great conversation with your kid in there.

Also, below are five different Parent Guides on different cultural challenges accelerated by the smartphone that your kid may face. They are about 10 pages each. We are including a free Parent's Guide to Sexting. We encourage you to read it, *even if* you think your kid would never sext. Knowledge is power. Or your could choose to visit axis.org to grab a different Parent Guide. They are only a few bucks.

Free Parent Guide Included with Smartphone Sanity:
Axis Parent's Guide to Sexting[41]

Other Parent Guides for Sale at Axis.org/Guides:
Axis Parent's Guide to Depression and Anxiety
Axis Parent's Guide to Pornography
Axis Parent's Guide to LGBT and Your Teen
Axis Parent's Guide to Suicide & Self-Harm Prevention

[41] Visit axis.org/sanity-sexting. If you haven't talked with your kid about sexting, now is the time. We believe in you!

18. Activity 2: Phone Forgiveness

Activity 2 is a unique chance to enter into your story with your kid. Are you ready? God made us to connect around story. Think of any great movie, book, or even a memorable campfire time you've been a part of. Stories are powerful no matter if they're small or big, fictional or true. *Your story is also powerful.*

Part of your story in this smartphone journey is to appropriately confess something to your kid that you have done or left undone in regard to your smartphone. By doing so, you invite your kid into your story. This does not look like spilling all your deep, dark secrets. Instead, it is honestly sharing a story of how you misuse your smartphone and even some of the why behind it. If you vulnerably invite them into this story (or stories), it will help them navigate both their own life and their inherited family narrative.

> *Stories are powerful no matter if they're small or big, fictional or true. Your story is also powerful. Don't let anyone tell you otherwise.*

But what does a confession like this look like? Well, it should have three parts. First is, "I'm sorry." Following that should be, "I was wrong." Lastly comes, "Will you forgive me?" A good confession needs all three components to fully show remorse, understanding, and a desire for reconciliation. If only one or two are incorporated, the confession or apology can be harmful instead of healing.

For example, "I'm sorry you thought I was wrong, will you forgive me," sounds accusatory. Or, "I was wrong, will you forgive me," leaves out the first person's emotional stake in the process. However, when all three components are present, it makes for a powerful relational connection.[42] Use this understanding to make the most of Activity 2!

EXPERIENCE: ACTIVITY 2!

The upcoming activity has you reflect on your own smartphone use![43] If you haven't yet done so, find a one hour spot on your family's calendar sometime soon for Activity 2. Again, there are three options for this experience. Do whichever you have time for!

1. Look, I'm Busy
2. You Can Do It!
3. The Overachiever Edition

WHAT'S THE ACTIVITY?

Experience: Make a fun meal together.
Story: Confess your failings in your smartphone use.
Blessing: Seek forgiveness and bless your kid.

Here's How It Works: You (the parents) will lead a family experience where you'll make a fun and simple meal with your kid (of any age). The goal during this time is to have an intentional conversation where you practice vulnerability with your son or daughter. This will set the stage for future conversations, because they will receive a **confession** from you. Wait, what?! Yes, we know it's scary, but isn't connection so much better than addiction? Remember what Johann Hari talked about? It's time to connect.

---

[42] Some vulnerability from me: Learning the simple three-step process needed in a proper apology changed my marriage. I love you, Lindsey! Thank you for being quick to forgive me! (Oh, FYI, Lindsey is my wife.)

[43] At the expense of being redundant . . . You've got a lot going on. Don't let these stress you out! Let this book serve you and skip the activities if you need to.

The goal of this time is for you to lead the way by confessing that you have areas where you can improve your smartphone usage. In leading by example you'll show that this needs to be an ongoing family conversation. **Vulnerability, humility, and a "shame-and-contempt-free" conversation is the way to go.** I will elaborate more on this in the upcoming chapters.

Do not imply your kids should also confess to you. This is about leading by example, they should not feel pressured to talk about themselves or confess to you. That's not the goal. The goal is your vulnerability.

OPTION 1: LOOK, I'M BUSY.

Step 1 and Done: Use Uber Eats or DoorDash and order a meal. Confess to your kids appropriately how you have misused your phone. Bam. Done.

OPTION 2: YOU CAN DO IT!

Step 1: *Plan a 1-2 hour window in your calendar* and make sure all your kids can make it (if possible).

Step 2: *Plan the meal.* Here's the key—it's not about the meal! The meal sets the stage for your confession and ensuing conversation. It provides you with an experience to surround with intentional conversation. The idea is to make this fun and simple. If you have a simple meal you can make together at home, that's perfect. Going to a new restaurant or someplace new that's conducive to conversation works too. Something that breaks the script of your family meals is a great way to make this memorable.

Step 3: *Prep for your confession.* This is by far the most important part. Do a smartphone fast for three hours sometime between now and Activity 2 and reflect during that time on these chapters about touch, addiction, shame, and the Five Pathologies (shame and the pathologies are addressed in the next chapters). Ask yourself why you're drawn to your phone in certain ways. Think about a way that you use your phone that you'd like to vulnerably confess to your kids. This is a great way to lead by example and show them that you're working on your smartphone use too. Once you know what you want to confess, think about this more deeply and identify **why** it is that you use your phone in this way.

(Is it loneliness, desire for success, a longing for companionship?) How you use your smartphone is really just a shadow of the real reason. Addiction and over-use stem from a deeper reason that makes you go to it as a "fix." **The why of your phone story is most important in your confession.** The root that you're willing to confess shows your kids that the surface is one thing, but the why is the ultimate thing to be aware of and discuss.

Confession Tips: Confessions seek to understand the why of a behavior and they have three parts. First, they involve sorrow for what has been done or left undone. "I'm sorry for _________." Second, there is a confession of wrongdoing. Just being sorry doesn't mean you believe you were wrong. It's important to say, "I was wrong for _________." Finally, it is important to ask for forgiveness. "Will you forgive me for _________?" Use all three to craft a full-bodied confession.

Step 4: *Have your family experience, and confess.* Find a moment while eating your meal for each parent to confess something about their smartphone use and what they think the deeper underlying issue is. **Tip:** Think through what you're going to say ahead of time. This should not be rehearsed, but it should be thought through. The key here is helping your kid see there's always a why behind a behavior or addiction. The point is for them to see that you're leading the way by looking at your own smartphone behavior before you ask them to look at theirs. **Do not ask for a confession from them.** By the way, if your kid doesn't have a phone yet, that doesn't make this confession any less important. It might even be more impactful. For your kid to see your smartphone confession when you don't yet have an agenda for them to change their behavior could be very powerful.

Conversation Tips: Be responsive and find connection. Be curious about their responses to your confession. Don't come across as judging, critiquing, or condemning. Be positive and have fun. Lastly, be appropriately serious with your confession, but not so serious that it sombers the mood.

OPTION 3: OVERACHIEVER EDITION

Step 1: Same instructions as Option 2.

Step 2: *For this extended experience, try making pizza at home!* Make this more fun and challenging by not grocery shopping beforehand. Just use whatever you happen to have in the fridge, buying only pizza dough. Sometimes the best recipes come out of using unexpected ingredients. It will either be delicious or super funny! The point is the meal you make together will be the experience you gather around to preface your conversation time with a unique family experience in your own kitchen.

Steps 3-4: Same instructions as Option 2. Be sure to look over the confession and conversation tips. Additionally, share your goals for your smartphone usage and/or a precaution you've taken in response to your phone use. These can be things like being on your phone only an hour a day, or something simple, like changing your display to grayscale. Show them you are taking action.

We hope these instructions help you on your way to a great confession with your kids! If you have any questions or confusions, feel free to reach out to us at axis.org. Use the chat box on our website—we are here to help.

STEP 3

boundaries

boundaries

19. Essential Conversation 3: We are on a Journey of Trust with a Destination of Independence.

20. Non-Negotiables, Money, Location, & Time

21. Internet & App Store

22. Texting & Social Media

23. Their Friend's Phone

24. Success Stories! & Social Media Case Study!

25. Activity 3: Hang Out with Your Friends

19. Essential Conversation 3: We are on a Journey of Trust with a Destination of Independence.

Welcome to Step Three: Boundaries! This step is dedicated to helping you know the ins and outs to the question, "How do I setup my kid's phone?" We actually had one mom ask us, "Can I just buy a phone and bring it by the Axis office so you can set it up for me?"[44]

So . . . instead of having her buy a plane ticket and drop by our office in Colorado we decided to write Step Three! This is the step many people have been waiting for where we will deliver all the tactical help needed for setting up your kid's phone.

> *Step Three contains all the tactical guidance you need to setup your kid's phone, but please be patient. You don't want to lose their heart.*

However, a quick word to the wise: You are going to want to take this power and use it, but please be patient! You don't want to lose your son or daughter's heart when you use this control; rather, you must invite them in to the process with you to foster trust, the foundation for our final step. Trust is exactly what we will be learning about now. Like always, this step starts with an exploration of the scriptural foundation for one of Axis' Four Essential Smartphone Conversations.

[44] True story. Don't you wish it was that easy?

Conversation 1: Very Good, Cursed, & Redeemed.
Conversation 2: What Is It For?
Conversation 3: We are on a Journey of Trust with a Destination of Independence.
Conversation 4: You Can Tell Me Anything!

The journey with your kid is a long one. From the excitement of the initial announcement "we're pregnant,"[45] to the intense birth, to the first haircut, to their first word, to dropping them off at kindergarten, to their first sport, to them hitting puberty, to their first phone . . . There are so many milestones in the journey!

So, have you ever wondered about Jesus' journey with his parents? It's a fun thought experiment to consider toddler-Jesus just learning to potty train, or to even ponder his first word! Which brings up a seldom-asked question, what *exactly* was Jesus' first word? Are you curious?

Well, of course we don't know what his first word was, but it very well might have been *Sh'ma*. According to the recorded oral Jewish laws in the Babylonian Talmud (Seder Mo'ed, Sukkah 42a) it is stated that a father was to teach his children the Torah and *Sh'ma*. You may know that the Torah is the first five books of the Old Testament. Less well known, however, is the term *Sh'ma. Sh'ma* simply means, "hear." It comes from a very famous passage in Deuteronomy 6:

> *Hear, O Israel: The Lord our God, the Lord is one. You shall love the Lord your God with all your heart and with all your soul and with all your might.*
>
> *And these words that I command you today shall be on your heart. You shall teach them diligently to your children, and shall talk of them when you sit in your house, and when you walk by the way, and when you lie down, and when you rise. You shall bind them as a sign on your hand, and they shall be as frontlets between your eyes. You shall write them on the doorposts of your house and on your gates.*
>
> — Deuteronomy 6:4-9

[45] The most hilarious video ever: axis.org/sanity-pregnant. Like, I ugly cry when I watch it, it's so hilarious. It's the video I showed the Axis team to announce that my third baby, Vale Calvary, was on his way.

Notice that when Jesus was asked what the greatest commandment was in the Gospel of Matthew, he just recited the *Sh'ma*. According to Deuteronomy 6, our parenting journey begins and ends with loving God with all that we are. Oh, and it's also the middle part, too. It's everything.

The third Essential Conversation is, "We are on a journey of trust with a destination of independence," and we can't forget that at every step of the way we are loving God with all that we are. There will be so many different conversations along the way when you are in your house, when you walk, when you are lying down, and when you rise. The *one conversation* is ongoing, repetitive, and often mundane, but so important. The instruction of a father and the teaching of a mother ultimately lead to life.

> *Hear, my son, your father's instruction,*
> *and forsake not your mother's teaching,*
> *for they are a graceful garland for your head*
> *and pendants for your neck.*
>
> — Proverbs 1:8–9

> *My son, keep your father's commandment,*
> *and forsake not your mother's teaching.*
> *Bind them on your heart always;*
> *tie them around your neck.*
> *When you walk, they will lead you;*
> *when you lie down, they will watch over you;*
> *and when you awake, they will talk with you.*
> *For the commandment is a lamp and the teaching a light, and the reproofs of discipline are the way of life.*
>
> — Proverbs 6:20–23

This "journey of trust with a destination of independence" is literally the "way of life" described at the end of the Scripture above. The "way of life" is forged from the loving correction and guidance from a father and mother. That's the path you want for your kids and it's the goal of *Smartphone Sanity*.

You don't want to be checking your kid's text messages indefinitely.

You want them to be independent; to have freedom; to know the way of life and to choose to walk it. In Step Three, where you will gain a lot of power and control, hold on to that power, thinking about the best way to implement it in the spirit of the *Sh'ma*—a way of life that hears and adheres to loving God with all that we are. As we begin Step Three we have a new blessing for you:

> *Hear, O Israel: The Lord our God, the Lord is one. You shall love the Lord your God with all your heart and with all your soul and with all your might.*
>
> *And these words that I command you today shall be on your heart. You shall teach them diligently to your children, and shall talk of them when you sit in your living room, and when you drive in your SUV to practice, and when you watch Netflix, and when you are late to school. You shall have them be the backdrop of your home-screen, and they shall be your profile on Snapchat. You shall place them on your refrigerator and hang them on your front door.*
>
> — Deuteronomy 6:4-9, Altered

20. Non-Negotiables, Money, Location, and Time

"So, your kids must love the iPad?" I asked Steve Jobs because the company's first tablet was just hitting the shelves. "They haven't used it," he told me. "We limit how much technology our kids use at home."

— Steve Jobs, Former CEO of Apple, NYT Interview

You're always looking at how technology can be used in a great way—homework and staying in touch with friends—and also where it has gotten to excess. We don't have cellphones at the table when we are having a meal, we didn't give our kids cell phones until they were 14 and they complained other kids got them earlier. We often set a time after which there is no screen time.

— Bill Gates, Founder of Microsoft

So, whether you eat or drink,
or whatever you do, do all to the glory of God.

— 1 Corinthians 10:31

Step Three's all about learning the manual and technical details for setting up your family's phones. **It'll be tempting to try to start implementing the 8 Smartphone Domains ASAP, but . . .**

DO NOT DO IT NOW![46]

[46] Overkill? Nah. Emphasis. ;)

The 8 Smartphone Domains

1. Non-Negotiables

No more non-negotiables.

- No illegal actions including driving laws about phones, etc.
- No bullying, or inappropriate (abusive) language.
- No porn, sexting, online dating, or "hook-up" apps.
- GPS location services are always on.
- Agreed family response times to calls & texts.
- No sneaky apps, hidden accounts, changing passwords, & no secrets.
- Parent will check phone frequently & know about every app.
- Parent has access to phone/apps at any time, has passcode, all passwords & logins, & can install software. There is no right to phone privacy.
- Phones are very good, cursed, & can be redeemed. God owns everything, & He owns all phones. Parents are responsible to God as the ultimate steward of the family phones.

2. Money

Your kid pays for everything.

- Who pays for the phone if/when it breaks?
- Who pays for phone cases & accessories?
- Who pays for apps, streaming music services, etc.
- Who pays for the phone plan & data?
- Who buys the phone? How often can it be upgraded?

3. Location

No policies for location.

<u>Policies while Away</u>:

- Friend's Homes
- Car
- Church
- School

<u>Policies for Home</u>:

- Sleeping
- Homework
- Meals
- Bathroom/Shower
- Bedroom

4. Time

No limits on time.

- Notification setup to minimize distractions.
- Scheduled downtime from phone.
- Specific app time limits.
- Total phone time limits.
- Tech Curfew PM to AM.
- Screen Time & Family Link. Native phone screen time control apps.
- Screen Time & Family Link. Native phone screen time awareness apps.

5. Internet

Allow native browser & App Store browsers.

Allow native browser. Turn on "limit adult content" in settings. No App Store browsers.

Allow native browser with whitelisted or blacklisted sites. On Android use "approve sites." Turn on "limit adult content" in settings. No App Store because of browsers.

No native browser. Install & pay for Covenant Eyes browser. Turn on filtering & reporting. Turn on "limit adult content" in settings. No App Store because of 3rd party browsers.

No native browser & no App Store for other browsers.

6. App Store

Allow App Store.

No "Family Sharing." No deleting apps setting. Limit adult content setting.

No "Family Sharing." No deleting apps setting. Limit adult content setting. Restrict apps based on ratings.

App Store with "Family Sharing" WITHOUT "Ask to Buy." No deleting apps setting. Limit adult content setting. Restrict apps based on ratings.

App Store with "Family Sharing" & "Ask to Buy." No deleting apps setting. Limit adult content setting.

Always know every app on their phone.

No App Store.

7. Texting

Allow texting.

Allow texting. Frequently monitor manually. Definitely pay for Bark.us reporting software. Bark will see deleted texts.

Allow texting. Mirror texts on a separate device or consider paying for a monitoring service like TeenSafe. Frequently monitor manually. Definitely pay for Bark.us reporting software.

No texting.

8. Social Media

Allow Social Media.

Multiple Social Media. Use Bark.us. Follow them & don't be a weirdo.

Allow multiple social media. Approve posts initially. Approve who they want to follow. Know login & password. Follow them but don't interact publicly. Login on occasion & look around. Use Bark.us.

Same as below except require approval for fewer posts.

Allow one social media. Approve all posts. Approve everyone they want to follow. Know login & password. Follow them but don't interact publicly. Login on occasion & look around. Use Bark.us.

No Social Media.

Just wait. We promise, it's better to not rush these changes without buy-in from your kids and spending time in prayer asking God for wisdom in how to implement them. **Rules without relationship result in rebellion.** The point of these is not controlling sin (aka behavior management), but instead using your phones to the glory of God! We are running toward the good, using our phones in a way that honors Him! The thing that is strange about Step Three's best practices is that they are a combination of manual and technical. All of these are suggestions, but we suggest you take each one of them seriously considering the strengths and weaknesses of your family, and . . . This is a big "AND . . . " **How you model these best practices and have honest conversations about them** will make all the difference. They should never feel like a power play. The Eight Domains we will discuss during Step Three and create a plan around in Step Four. It may look like a lot, but you've got what it takes.

> *How you model these best practices and have honest conversations about them will make all the difference. Rules without relationship result in rebellion.*

DOMAIN 1: NON-NEGOTIABLES

These non-negotiables have to do with your kid's access to a phone. (Note: We will cover *moral non-negotiables* during Step Four in the Moral Compass chapter.)

PHONE OWNERSHIP

God owns your phones and you and your kids steward them. The phone is never *their* phone. Even if you "give" your kid a phone for their birthday or a holiday . . . it is still *your* phone. They are just leasing it. **Be obnoxiously clear about that.** Remember, it's their borrowed phone, or their family phone, not actually "their" phone.

PRIVACY

There is no such thing as phone privacy. Especially when you are young and developing, still learning how to use technology in a healthy way. Additionally, there is *definitely* no claim to privacy when the phone they use is yours. Again, be obnoxiously clear about the implications of that!

PRE-SMARTPHONE DUMBPHONE

If you haven't gotten your kid a smartphone yet, consider the other options on the market that will meet your needs. Just going to a store to buy a flip phone is not as easy as you may think. Flip phones often cost as much as smartphones! Yet, there are many devices that will allow you to call, text, and follow the GPS of your kid without having to get them a full-on smartphone. Check out the DokiWatch for younger kids, or the YipYap phone. Also consider the Relay phone, designed to keep you in touch in a new way . . . a screen-free smartphone! You may even consider the Light Phone II for older students. A very promising phone is the Gabb phone, but time will tell. Or you could always resort to smoke-signals, if you're desperate.

As you consider getting a more standard smartphone, we highly recommend Republic Wireless. Most plans are not unlimited (a little scarcity is good) and they utilize a technology that uses mostly WiFi calling, although if you are away from WiFi it easily taps into normal cellular networks. And the plans are almost half-price!

APPLE ID OR GOOGLE LOGIN & PASSWORD

Initially, only you should know the login and password for the main ID (AppleID or Google Login). The password should be complex; for protection and so your kid cannot easily guess it. Eventually, parents can let their kid know the login and password as their trust grows. For Android users, if your kid is younger than 13, then their account must be bound to a parent account. You should still know their account and password, but they can know it too since you will have parental controls.

PHONE ACCESS

You should have access to your kid's phone at any time to see what they are doing. And you will have access to all usernames and passwords for every app. You can take away the phone whenever you want and you can setup any visibility app that you deem appropriate. Like we said above, there is no such thing as phone privacy. This will feel like a lot of power. Use it gently.

PHONE DISCIPLINE

If/When you take away the phone it will not be indefinite, unless you tell them you just took a job in the tundra of Siberia. Then yes, they will not need a phone. Seriously, when you take the phone away, tell them when they will get it back. If the offense is severe, sell the smartphone and get them a dumbphone. They will have to manage a new social life without a phone for however long they don't have it. And remember, as always, you will be fair.

DOMAIN 2: MONEY

BUYING A PHONE & UPGRADES

So you have made the bold decision . . . you are going to let your kid have a phone! Your kid hires a mariachi band to celebrate and everyone in your family is doing the happy dance. Congratulations, you are no longer a fascist[47] and your kid is NOT the ONLY kid without a phone anymore. Wahoo! But, wait a second. Who is paying for this $1,000 pocket rectangle? Dang. I knew there was a catch.

We've seen everything at Axis. Some parents just buy their kid a phone, others make them pay for it, some buy the minimum and let their kid upgrade it, still others split the cost. What will you do? It's good to figure out and communicate with your kid before they spend their phone money hiring a mariachi band. And even if they do buy it with their own money, if they are living under your roof, you still "own" it.[48] At risk of quoting my dad, it's hard to value something you aren't paying for.

---

47 I'm foreshadowing the next chapter. Get excited.

48 Remember, next chapter we are discussing fascism.

PHONE UPGRADES

Oh, you thought we were done talking about money? Not quite yet. We still have a few pages to go. Ok, it's time to get serious. Your kid will be *bullied* if they have an old phone or no phone. I remember my good friend's son weeping hot tears because he had a "little kid" phone. All he wanted was a phone that wasn't a few years old. Please, have empathy for this. Junior High and High School is a jungle. It's survival of the coolest. Yet, stick to your convictions. Your kid doesn't need the newest, coolest, best-est phone . . . but if they don't have it you must prepare them for the challenges they may face navigating the adolescent wilderness.

It's a lot like the first car we each drove years ago. Remember that? I do. And I don't like remembering it.[49] It's a good idea to consider how often you will pay, or allow your kid to pay, to upgrade their phone.

MONTHLY PLAN & DATA

Hey, would you like to keep talking about money? Let's do it. Once the up front cost is paid there is now the monthly cost of the phone plan. Who will pay for that plan and how will the cost be split, and how will the family share the data? Luckily a lot of plans now include unlimited data, although there are always caveats. Be aware and make a plan.

BUYING APPS, ETC.

Now, the App Store. Some of the most profitable apps are free-to-play, but have in app upgrades. Some have monthly subscriptions. Some cost money once. Will your kid have an app allowance? How will you handle this digital invisible currency?

Another friend of mine noticed a strange line-item on his credit card bill for over a thousand dollars. Upon research his son quickly confessed, he had spent ONE THOUSAND DOLLARS[50] on in-app purchases to upgrade one of his apps. Yes, the app was categorized as "free-to-play." Thankfully this kid has a great, incredibly patient dad.[51]

---

[49] I bought a Chevy Lumina for $200 one time. It was good for the first 10 miles, then it overheated. Luckily my first job was only 15 miles away.

[50] The cost of 5 Chevy Luminas in 2006 . . .

[51] The son's indentured servitude is almost paid off. Only a decade left.

CASES & ACCESSORIES

Next, will there be a case? Will there be multiple cases to match different outfits? Will there be upgraded Air Pods? Who will pay for these? Another great thing to talk about.

IT'S GOING TO BREAK & SOMEONE MUST PAY

Can we just take a moment to celebrate that phones are now waterproof? I've had so many friends who have dropped their phones in the toilet and then proceeded to set their phones in a bowl of dry rice. Thanks be to God that era is over.

I've smashed at least three phones (on accident, of course!). They are expensive to fix. And if you pay for the insurance, that is expensive too. Who will pay for a new phone when it breaks? Create answers to these questions now. When disaster strikes, you'll be so glad you did.

DOMAIN 3: LOCATION

SCHOOL

Having a phone at school is completely up to you. Usually this is one of the first reasons parents get their kid a phone, especially with the increase in school violence. Certain built-in features and apps (which we will detail in the Phone Setup Guide section) will allow you to pause certain apps during school hours so that your student is less distracted at school.

YOUR HOME

Oh, and by the way, these rules do not just apply to your kid, but any kids under your supervision. Your kid's friends may have different rules at home; but, while they are in your home, they have to follow your rules, too.

HOMEWORK

You may have a good idea of how distracting a phone is to your kid during homework by reflecting on how it can distract you at work. Many families choose no phones during homework, or they use a screen time limiting app to remove distractions. Again, expect to hear about that in the Phone Setup Guide section soon. Also, keep in mind there are a lot of great ways to use your phone to help with homework or to connect with other students to collaborate.

DINNER

Breaking bread together as a family builds incredible community . . . unless there are phones present. Consider stacking all phones in the center of the table during dinner . . . or even better, have them in another room. Just the presence of a phone will distract you from being fully present in that moment.

BEDROOMS

We strongly suggest no phones in bedrooms ever. Phones give the illusion of privacy even when you are in public. Having them privately in bedrooms opens an entirely new Pandora's box. Expect your teen to sleep 1 or 2 hours less a night if the phone is in their bedroom.

BATHROOM/SHOWER

This is up to you and really depends on the level of visibility (monitoring and filtering) you have of your kid's phone. Many phones are currently water resistant. (The iPhone X is rated IP67, meaning that it is completely dust-resistant and water-resistant when submerged at a depth of 1 meter or less for up to 30 minutes) Therefore, they will want to take the phone with them into the shower, so a decision needs to be made. Bedrooms and bathrooms/showers should be treated in a similar way.

CHURCH

Consider bringing physical Bibles to church and leaving the phones in the car. Yes, there are amazing Bible study tools that we can access on our phones; however, there is also a universe of distractions. Let church be sacred from those distractions.

DRIVING

This again is up to you. Distracted driving may be the new drunk driving. Texting is illegal in many states and talking on the phone is illegal in some as well. Obviously, you should obey the laws, but safety is an important issue for family discussion even if your state doesn't have these laws. There are apps that recognize when you are driving and pause some of the phone's features.

DOMAIN 4: TIME

PHONE CURFEW FROM PM TO AM

Decide on a phone curfew for the weekdays and another for the weekends. After curfew, all phones (and tablets etc.) are put away in a common area (not bedrooms) to charge. This works best if you participate as well, and there will be some rare occasions where you all will break the rules. Consider setting a gentle alarm that goes off every evening at the start time. One of the best tricks for this is assigning a start and end time. You don't want your daughter getting up at 5:30am to immediately start managing her social media. (There are apps that can help with this too . . . more soon, we promise!)

PHONE CHARGING AT NIGHT

To be redundant, find a common area for phones to charge at night. Yes, it is possible for your kids to sleep without them. No, they don't have to have a phone for an alarm (just buy an alarm clock, like one of the experiences from Step Two). And, no they don't need music from a smartphone to fall asleep. This is a fact: If they don't have a phone in their room, they will sleep better. And teenagers need their sleep!

TIME LIMITS

Consider setting limits for screen time on weekdays and weekends, otherwise phones will do what they were designed to do . . . captivate everyone's attention. Again, there are apps that can help with this. In thinking about limiting your kid's screen time, remember to control your own. This chapter's experience focuses on helping you control your own screen time. The Phone Setup Guide below has all the ways you can control your kid's screen time. Lead by example, and start with these 7 Simple Practices. Then, read how you have a lot of power over their screen time in the following Phone Setup Guide.

EXPERIENCE: 7 SIMPLE PRACTICES TO BE PRESENT

Here are some simple tools you can use on **your** phone to help you be more present. Try a few of them, depending on the occasion, to engage with the people around you. Your kids will notice, we promise!

ONE: RED DOT INVENTORY

Do an inventory of the "red dots" on your phone, also known as notifications. Consider turning off all non-human notifications; and, especially if you use it for work, turn-off email notifications!

TWO: DO NOT DISTURB

A simple tool that turns off notifications and phone calls during hours you set. You can also set it to receive calls from specific phone numbers (your family), or people who call twice in a row in the rare case of an emergency.

THREE: OUT OF SIGHT

Put your phone in another room, or even in a drawer in another room, or even in a lead box in a drawer in another room. Or just be "that parent" and buy a military-grade Faraday pouch online and put your phone in it, your kid's phone, and your kid's friend's phone when they visit.

FOUR: AIRPLANE MODE

When using "Airplane Mode," your phone is still on, but it is much harder for you to be distracted by the people who text you, or the non-human notifications that are begging for your attention. Remember, if you are not paying for the app or social media, you are not the customer. **You are the product being sold.**

> *If you are not paying for the app or social media, you are not the customer. You are the product being sold.*

FIVE: POWER BUTTON

You guessed it. Just turn it off.

You'd be surprised at how this clears your heart so you can be fully present with the people you are around.

SIX: LEAVING THE PHONE AT HOME

This is the ultimate. Just leave your phone at home when you go to visit a friend or go out to dinner. There is a strange freedom that will come over you. It is slightly warm. You'll like it.

SEVEN: MOVE TO SIBERIA

That would do the trick. Or you could move to where my folks live in Texas. Different temperatures. Similar phone experience.

Phone Setup Guide!
Screen Time Awareness and Control

Your first dose of power! Remember Uncle Ben's wise words—with great power, comes great responsibility.[52]

In this section we are covering Screen Time Awareness and Control. Please know that **no system is perfect**, but we think you will still be impressed with some of the options that are out there. This is your power, and using it in love and mercy is your responsibility. **Remember, rules without relationship result in rebellion.**

SO, WHAT IS SCREEN TIME AWARENESS?

Screen time awareness is your ability to measure the amount of time your kid has spent on "their" phone and measures the amount of time spent in each app.

THEN, WHAT IS SCREEN TIME CONTROL?

Screen time control is the ability to control, remotely (from your phone) or by passcode (protected settings on their phone), many functions on "their" phone. This section will tell you how to do these two things for iPhone or Android phones. Skip to the section appropriate for you. Note: Our world is ever-changing, and technology changes fast. If you find any of the below material to have changed since the printing of this book, chat us up at axis.org. We probably have an answer for you, or if not we will find one.

iPhone: Phone Setup Guide[53]
Screen Time Awareness and Control

The software on your iPhone now features a new Screen Time App that offers a full analysis ON _your phone_ ABOUT _your kid's phone_. This includes information about apps used, the number of notifications received, the

52 Spidey inspiration here: axis.org/sanity-ben.
53 No iPhone? Skip to the Android section!

number of times the phone was picked up, and other features. It will also allow you to control the amount of time they spend on their phone and their phone bedtime curfew. (Remember, it is your phone, and they are learning to use it under your supervision. It is *not* "their phone.")

So first, install that update you've been putting off! It's worth its figurative weight in gold. Until you do, you can still check their screen time by going to Settings >> Battery. Click the small clock icon next to the "Last 7 Days" button. Then you can see the amount of time spent on apps for the "Last 24 Hours" or the "Last 7 Days." Once you have the newest iOS downloaded and installed, you will need to set-up Screen Time on your kid's phone. There are two ways to do this.

The first way is with their phone in hand. On their phone, go to Settings > > Screen Time. It will prompt you with a set-up screen, so choose "Continue," and select, "This is my child's phone." (If it does not prompt you with a set-up screen, scroll down and find "Turn Off Screen Time" in red ink. Select it, confirm, and return to Settings. Then, open Screen Time again and it should give you a set-up screen.) If you are setting up a brand-new iPhone for your kid, go through the start-up process and create an Apple ID for them. Then choose "Continue" when prompted to set up Screen Time. After the set-up process, go to Settings and follow the instructions above to turn on Screen Time.

The other way to set up Screen Time is through Family Sharing. Go to Settings > > Family Sharing **on your phone** and add your kid as a family member with their Apple ID and password. Then select Screen Time, your kid's account, and "Turn Screen Time On." One important thing: If you ever take them out of Family Sharing, your restrictions will be lifted.

After either way of setting up Screen Time, you can now choose all sorts of restrictions, starting with "Downtime" and "App Limits," which both enforce screen time awareness and control. Create a passcode that your kid will not be able to guess, one they cannot easily find out when you enter it for them. This passcode will lock all changes in the Screen Time app, and also will lock the phone from a "factory reset," which would erase all restrictions you set. Beware, if you choose to turn off Screen Time, you will erase all your restrictions. If you want to give your kid more time on their phone or a particular app, do not turn off Screen Time. Instead, enter your passcode on their phone for the app for which you are granting more time.

Lastly, in Screen Time, choose which apps you want to always allow —regardless of screen time limits—in case of emergencies. For example, the phone function cannot be disabled, along with any others you add to the list. This is not just for emergencies. If you want your kid to have limited time on Instagram, but to always be able to access their Kindle app, you can put that app here.

Android: Phone Setup Guide [54] [55] [56] Screen Time Awareness and Control

Android screen time awareness and control feature is the Google Family Link app. If your kid has an Android phone, the Family Link app allows you to be aware of their total screen time, track their individual app time, and control their phone from your Android *or* iPhone.

It costs NOTHING. It is also creepy how simple it is to set up. You will need to have access to your kid's phone to set it up.

First, download the Google Family Link app from the App Store or the Family Link Manager App from the Google Play Store **on your phone**. When you open the app, it will run you through an orientation to ensure you have everything you need to set up the account.

Then, it will prompt you to create a Google account for your kid. One weird Google rule: Family Link only works with Google accounts for children under 13 (or the relevant age as determined by applicable law in your jurisdiction). Once a child turns 13, they can continue to use Family Link if they choose to do so. You might have to adjust the age that you report to Google about your child, *wink wink*.

To create an account, first create an email for them, and then a password, both of which they will know. Google ensures you are actually a parent by requiring a credit card number. They do not charge anything through Family Link, and your kid will not have access to your payment information. After making sure you have the correct set-up

54 Don't have an Android? Lucky you!
55 I'm kidding.
56 Or am I?

and then creating your kid's Google account, it is finally time to connect to your kid's phone.

If you are setting up a **new** Android phone for your kid, follow the set-up instructions. When prompted for a Google account, set up a new one for your kid (under age 13). **If you just made one for them in Family Link, use that account.** Finish the rest of the set-up, in which you will download Family Link from the Google Play Store on your kid's phone. You will then choose which apps to limit, along with other restrictions as prompted by the set-up program.

If you are trying to set up Family Link on an existing Android phone, chances are your kid already has a Google account. If they are under 13 and have an account that is not under your parent account, they likely lied about their age to set up their account (since Google forces parent supervision to create an account for ages under 13). If they are older than 13, then Family Link won't do you much good, unfortunately. You can invite them to your family (and they will have to accept through an email they receive), **but you won't be able to manage anything on their phone once they join unless you report a younger age for them to Google.**

Once you have set up a Family Link connection on your kid's phone, go back to your phone and open Family Link. Go to the tab in the app for your kid's phone and start setting the restrictions you see fit. The sections on "Screen Time" and "Daily Limits" are particularly relevant, as well as setting a "Bedtime" when the phone will lock automatically.

"

No system is perfect,
but some of the
new tools available
are truly incredible.

"

21. Internet & App Store

> *This is rule No. 1: There are no screens in the bedroom. Period. Ever. My kids accuse me and my wife of being fascists*[57] *and overly concerned about tech, and they say that none of their friends have the same rules. We have rules because we have seen the dangers of technology firsthand. I've seen it in myself, I don't want to see that happen to my kids.*
>
> — Chris Anderson, Editor of Wired Magazine

> *Children, obey your parents in the Lord, for this is right. "Honor your father and mother"—which is the first commandment with a promise— "so that it may go well with you and that you may enjoy long life on the earth." Fathers, do not exasperate your children; instead, bring them up in the discipline and instruction of the Lord.*
>
> — Ephesians 6:1-4

Now we're getting technical, and it will be a bit of heavy reading. We are specifically looking at two different Pandora's Boxes included on smartphones: Internet Browsers and the App Store. You'll be glad to have this content, though, because this is the moment that many of you have been waiting for . . .

. . . but as we dig in, a short thought on the passage in Ephesians. Everything that we are about to show you is to equip you to help your kids have things "go well" so that they "enjoy long life on earth." ***This is all about LIFE.*** Enjoying long life. It's not about the rules. The rules

[57] Impressive failed negotiation attempt.

serve something bigger. They serve LIFE. And ultimately abundant life. Life to the full.

Also the rules you will create are not a trump card to overwhelm, overpower, and exasperate your kids.

Just like the last chapter, at the end of this section we have attached the Phone Setup Guide. It will contain everything you need to know to fully control your kid's phone.

But first you may want to know why you need to put boundaries on them: **sneaks and dangers.**

> *The rules serve something bigger. They serve life.*

DOMAIN 5: INTERNET (WITH SNEAKS)

NATIVE BROWSERS

Safari is the native browser for iPhone and Chrome is the native browser for Android. Out of the box these are both "on" and have full access to everything on the internet. And by everything we mean *everything*.

PRIVATE BROWSING, AKA PORN MODE

Safari has "private browsing" and Chrome has "incognito mode." These modes are included inside each browser and automatically forget the pages you visit, erase your search history, ignore auto-fill, and don't download any cookies.

OTHER BROWSERS

Other browsers are available in the App Store and Google Play store and they can be easily downloaded for free. They, too, have full access to the internet and private browsing. Firefox, Opera, and Microsoft Edge are some of the popular ones. There are also apps designed specifically for private browsing, like the Private Browsing web browser app. Again, all history, cookies, cache, etc. are completely deleted when you exit these apps when they are in private mode.

SNEAKY BROWSERS

There are apps like the Fake Calculator app and the Secret Calculator app that look and function like real calculators. Even their app logos on the phone's screen look like calculators. However, if you know the secret numerical code, the app opens up a hidden database for your kid to put photos and videos in. It also has a secret browser that is available.

ACCESSING BROWSERS WITH NON-BROWSER APPS

Other apps have access to the internet and can therefore get access to an internet browser. For example, Google Maps. You can search for the Google headquarters inside Google Maps. It will take you to a landing page for Googleplex in Mountain View, CA. From there you can access Google's homepage, google.com. And now you are on the internet unfettered. From other apps you can click the Twitter social media icon. This will take you to Twitter. From Twitter you can search for Google. From the Google page on Twitter you can click google.com and thus gain unfettered access. Not all apps will give you access but many will.

VPN BROWSERS

A Virtual Private Network (VPN) redirects your connection to the Internet via a remote server run by a VPN provider. This way, the VPN server becomes a secure launching pad for you before you access various websites. As far as websites are concerned, you're browsing from the server's geographical location, not your computer's location, aka your IP address. This allows you to: 1. Protect against cyber criminals over low-security networks. 2. Enhance privacy by hiding online activities from your Internet Service Provider (ISP). This way, the ISP cannot pass your private information to third parties, such as advertisers or government. 3. Lastly it can also be used to bypass internet censorship set up by a school, workplace, or ISPs.

SEARCH HISTORY, COOKIES, CACHE

In the settings for your native browsers on your phone you can frequently hit the button "Clear History and Website Data" to remove tracking.

WEBPAGES OF NATIVE APPS

Many apps that are popular in their native app version also have a web-app version that is accessible via an internet browser. Even if you have no access to the Facebook app you can have access to it via a webpage. The same is true with Twitter. Instagram does not allow you to post from the internet but you can view it. Snapchat only works in its native app, for now. Many apps have web functionality.

CHANGE THE CLOCK

Sometimes this works and sometimes it doesn't. It just depends on the operating system and how far it has been updated. Say you put a restriction on your kid's phone from 8pm to 8am. After 8pm they can go into their clock setting and set to clock to believe it is actually 5pm so that they get 3 more hours of phone time! Like we said . . . this was a big sneak in the past . . . and is currently mostly fixed. But perhaps not everywhere.

SCREEN RECORDING THE PASSCODE

Some apps allow you to record what happens on a phone's screen. Think of it like a video version of a screenshot. Therefore kids will turn on a screen recorder then hand their parent their phone so that the parent can unlock the phone with a passcode. They now have a video of the passcode, and they will use it—unbeknownst to their parent—to unlock and re-lock the phone when needed.

WIFI HOTSPOT

They may be locked out of internet apps on their phone and the home WiFi may be shut off; but, they can use their phone's WiFi hotspot to give their other devices (iPad, laptop, etc.) internet access.

"BORROW" YOUR PARENTS PHONE WHILE THEY SLEEP

Many families charge their phones in a common area like a kitchen or entryway. Although the student may be locked out of their phone they can easily sneak into the kitchen and "borrow" your phone while you sleep to browse the internet.

USING THEIR FRIEND'S OLD PHONE (AKA: THE BURNER PHONE BLACK MARKET)

Finally, if they have limits on their phone, they may buy or be given their friends old phone when that friend gets an upgrade. They will then hide this phone from you so that they can do whatever they want on their secret phone. Even without cell service this phone can do a lot on your WiFi. Most schools have a black market for these phones. What is our world coming to? Sheesh.

DOMAIN 6: APP STORE (WITH SNEAKS)

DOWNLOAD, DELETE, AND REPEAT

Why would anyone prevent their kid from deleting apps? Well, in the worst-case scenario, your kid can download an app on-demand, use it, and then delete it to make sure you didn't know they ever had it. Then repeat.

SNEAKY APPS

Like the Secret Calculator mentioned above there are apps designed to deceive parents. The way you can tell the difference is by looking at what the actual app promises in the App Store or Google Play. Also check the reviews for people to call-out the app for what it *really* does. Do your best to know every app on their phone.

APPS HIDDEN A FEW FOLDERS DEEP

You can also put apps deep inside folders where a parent's eyes might not look. We heard one story of some parents who grounded their son from Instagram and made him delete it. A few weeks later, at a dinner party, they were sharing how good he has been since deleting Instagram. The other parents at the party were confused, because they had been seeing the son's posts for weeks. He was still on Instagram, he had just hidden the app a few folders deep!

INVISIBLE FOLDERS

Similarly, it is possible to create a transparent folder inside another transparent folder. This makes it look like there is no folder on your phone's screen so you can hide apps in there. However, a list of all apps will be in the phone's settings.

APPS YOU CAN'T MONITOR

When your kid is actually in an app it is very hard to monitor their activity. Some VPN monitoring software (like Covenant Eyes) will allow you to see high level domain names for websites they have visited inside each app, but that is about it.

APPS WITH DIRECT MESSAGING, AKA PRIVATE MESSAGING YOU CAN'T MONITOR

Many apps allow for Direct Messaging. These are private and unless you are logged into the app you cannot see them. Still some apps automatically delete these messages or allow the user to delete them. This is another level of sneak . . . it's not just app activity you can't monitor, but the in-app communications, too!

SHARED DANGERS: INTERNET & APP STORE

AFFINITY GROUPS

A father once told us he was 100% sure his daughter was gender-fluid because of the internet. The internet is filled with affinity groups made up of groups of like-minded people. You have fans of a common sports teams in one affinity group, serious players of Settlers of Catan in another group, and Lord of the Rings fans in another group. However, on the darker side you can have Pro-Ana affinity groups made of people who will encourage you to meet your Anorexia goals. Or LGBT+ groups that will give your teen a community to get advice about how to determine if they are same-sex attracted.

DESTRUCTIVE BEHAVIOR

You can find ways to kill yourself, make bombs, find drugs, etc. And that's just the tip of the iceberg, unfortunately.

DARK WEB

The dark web is the World Wide Web content that exists on darknets, overlay networks that use the internet but require specific software, configurations, or authorization to access. The dark web forms a small part of the deep web, the part of the web not indexed by web search engines. It is usually a very dark and unsafe place. Think Knockturn Alley from Harry Potter, but real, and dark ,and dangerous. How wicked can it become? This is the place where child porn is trafficked.

PREDATORS

No longer does a predator have to volunteer in person at venues that have younger children. Instead they can "catfish" (lure someone into a relationship by means of a fictional online persona) online by acting like a 14-year old. Predators will then commence to "groom" their prey and encourage them to meet with them IRL (in real life).[58]

PORNOGRAPHY

There are so many issues to bring up about the dangers of porn. Here are some clear dangers, just to name a few:

- ***Online and Free.*** XXX is AAA. Affordable, Accessible, and Anonymous. This is a big change from the days you had to go to a seedy part of town and purchase porn from another human being or even receiving a pornographic magazine in the mail.
- ***Porn of Everything.*** Another rule of thumb is that there is porn of everything. It targets consumers of every predisposition and interest.
- ***Addictive and Unsatisfying.*** Porn creates addiction and drives the consumer to more extreme and violent versions of porn for the same high. Consider watching our Axis video Conversation Kit about pornography to see how porn promises satisfaction, purpose, and freedom, but really delivers addiction, lost identity, and slavery. You don't have to feel uncomfortable—our video Conversation Kit is completely tasteful but still addresses the issue head on, and it is just a few bucks at axis.org.
- ***Porn and the Brain.*** Porn creates a chemical addiction that can't be

[58] Ready to freak out? Ready to freak your kid out? Watch the video at axis.org/sanity-catfish with them to see how easy it is to be catfished. Very scary and enlightening. Might be worth watching by yourself first.

cleared out of your bloodstream like heroin or cocaine.

- ***Encourages Meeting with Strangers.*** Porn is never enough and porn websites know this. The websites encourage users to meet with strangers for sexual encounters.
- ***Predators.*** Speaking of meeting with strangers, predators will seek your kid out on porn websites, groom them, and encourage a meeting in real life. This is terrifying.
- ***Oh, and It's All a Lie.*** And, it's worth noting . . . these are paid actors faking intimacy. Those videos will pervert anyone's understanding of intimacy.
- ***Sex Trafficking.*** Yes, porn fuels the sex-trafficking industry.
- ***It's a Slippery Slope.*** A first viewing of porn (usually accidental) takes away innocence. After that it can easily slide to intentional searching because of its addictive nature. Therefore you must talk with your kid when they are young before they normally (50 years ago) would have been ready to learn about sex. This is a loss of innocence that is mandatory to protect them because what you talk about with them, they will talk about with you. You must frame the conversation first if you can. Second, there is a huge chance they will accidentally view porn and they need to know you are a safe person to tell about that. Third, strengthen your heart! There could be times they will intentionally pursue porn. You need to be ready to pursue their heart during these times. Pray for them, weep over them, and invite them into a truer, richer, more life-giving understanding of sexuality that the Bible offers.

> *"If you don't disciple your kid, the pornography industry is eager to mentor them."*

With all the due-diligence you can do a pretty decent job of setting up your kid's phone for success. However, where there is a will, there is a way. There are ways to access porn on your desktop, laptop, tablet, gaming systems, and your TVs. Even on dumbphones. Sickening, we know. There are solutions for all of these access points, we just aren't covering them in this book. Always think about three things:

1. Where does your home WiFi come from and is it filtered?
2. Is there monitoring on all your devices that have data?
3. Do you talk about this all the time in a safe way?

WELL, NOW I'M SCARED

Not our goal. Take some deep breaths. Or just go break something. But do not grab your kid's phone and start implementing the power we show you next. Below in the Phone Setup Guide are all the controls you are probably itching to enforce on your kid's phone; however, let's try a little experimentation with your own phone first.

EXPERIENCE: TRY IT ON YOURSELF

Below we've given you all the tools you need to brainwash your kid's phone. But first, we want you to try it on your phone. This way you can know how to set it up and how it works before you start messing with their phone. Once you set some restrictions, try being sneaky! See if you can break the restrictions you set or find any holes in the software. We think you will be happy with how frustratingly thorough most of the restrictions are!

Phone Setup Guide! Parental Controls

Power will intoxicate the best hearts, as wine the strongest heads. No man is wise enough, nor good enough to be trusted with unlimited power.

— Charles Caleb Colton

Your kid should not have unlimited power over their phone when they first get one. Parental Controls are native (built-in) in smartphones that can be toggled on or off to safeguard or limit certain apps. Once settings are toggled, a parent can set a passcode to keep their kid from changing them. Use your power wisely and in community with your spouse or other parents. We have options for both iPhone and Android. Pick the one that you need and skip the other!

iPhone: Phone Setup Guide Parental Controls[59]

Again, you need iOS 12 or later and Screen Time to do anything big in this arena. Download and install it now! All the parental controls can be found in the Settings App under Screen Time, specifically in the Content and Privacy Restrictions tab. Since we dealt with Downtime, App Limits, and Always Allowed with screen time awareness and control, all that's left is Content and Privacy Restrictions. First, toggle restrictions to "On." Now there will be 3 content categories and 11 privacy categories, along with 7 areas where you can lock your changes. We will take you through these one by one.

ITUNES AND APP STORE PURCHASES

Here you can disallow installing apps, deleting apps, or simply purchasing apps. Also, note that you can require a password for purchases, allowing only authorized users to buy apps. This blocks

59 Prefer to see pictures? Visit axis.org/sanity-protect and we will send you to our friend's site at Protect Young Eyes for a step-by-step visual walk through.

friends and others who would not know the password from downloading anything.

ALLOWED APPS

Under this category you can toggle off any pre-installed apps, such as Safari or the iTunes Store. This means that if your kid is not yet ready for the responsibility of the internet or the App Store (among other things) you can turn them off.

CONTENT RESTRICTIONS

In this tab, you can set rating limitations for everything: music, podcasts, news, movies, TV shows, books, apps, Siri, game center, and even web content and language. (One note on books: Just because they are a good alternative to games does not mean you should not filter them. You will definitely want to restrict sexually explicit books because of the proliferation of erotica.) Note that under Web Content you have three options: unrestricted access, limit adult content, and allowed websites only. This last option allows your kid to only access websites from a list you can customize.

LOCATION SERVICES, SHARE MY LOCATION

You can turn on Location Services so you can always access your kid's location via your phone. You can also decide whether or not to allow Share my Location, which works through the messaging app. Additionally, you can lock these changes so they remain as you have chosen. This built-in feature will show you their real-time location. Also, the Life 360 App allows you to see where they have been. This works great unless they leave their phone somewhere purposely to trick you. Remember, it's all about the relationship!

CONTACTS

Here you can control the apps that have asked to use your kid's contact list. Obviously, this is an important area to be vigilant for sketchy messaging apps. You can also lock the changes you make here.

CALENDARS, REMINDERS, PHOTOS, BLUETOOTH SHARING, MICROPHONE, SPEECH RECOGNITION, MEDIA & APPLE MUSIC

These sections are less of a threat, but if you should ever need to control which apps use these tools, here is where you do so. There may be no apps wanting to use these tools, but it's a good idea to just check what's asking for access every once in a while. You can lock your changes to these categories as well.

ADVERTISING

Here you can choose whether to allow ads or not. This is particularly useful if your kid plays app games that may have many ads throughout the play experience, which can be distracting, annoying, or lead to games/sites of which you would not approve.

PASSCODE CHANGES AND ACCOUNT CHANGES

In these sections, you can lock the passcode and account your kid uses so that they cannot add or change any passwords or account information.

CELLULAR DATA CHANGES

In this tab you can make it so cellular data cannot be turned off. Sometimes it is useful to be able to turn it off, so you can save data when using WiFi. However, if you have a problem with your kid turning it off and leaving it off, you can make it so it always stays on. Or, a problem with them turning it off to use unfiltered WiFi . . .

VOLUME LIMIT

All you can do here is either allow changes to the volume limit, or lock it. To change the volume limit, go to Settings > > Music and select Volume Limit. So, if you're worried your teen is listening to Tay Tay too loud on their AirPods, this will set the max volume that can be reached in their headphones or on the main phone speaker.

DO NOT DISTURB WHILE DRIVING

Similar to the volume limit, all you can do here is either allow Do Not Disturb While Driving, or disallow it. To set-up Do Not Disturb While Driving, go to Settings > > Do Not Disturb and scroll down to the bottom section on driving.

TV PROVIDER AND BACKGROUND APP ACTIVITIES

These categories may not be the most helpful, but if you need to adjust the TV provider settings on your kid's phone (if you have one), or disallow apps to run in the background (some apps function this way), then here is where you go.

Android: Phone Setup Guide[60] Parental Controls

What joy! All of these controls can be accessed and toggled from the Google Family Link app! Let's do it. Open the Family Link app from YOUR phone (iPhone or Android) and click your kid's tab. Select "Choose Settings."

CONTROLS ON GOOGLE PLAY

Require Approval for All Content . . . um, YES. Shall we digress a bit on the topic of Google Play? Let's digress. The apps in Google Play are like Pandora's Box. On it you have access to other internet browsers, other apps with access to the internet indirectly, social media, and many, many other apps. As a parent, we believe you should know every app on your kid's phone and ask, "What is it for?" A potentially tedious part of your life will be approving apps and talking about what they are for. Amazingly, on Google Play they are as easy to remove as they are to add.

RATINGS

Here you can set ratings according to your kid's level of maturity in the following categories: apps & games, movies, TV, books (you'll definitely

60 I showed these controls to my friend. Let's say his name is Darby. He loved the "God-like powers" he had over his kid's phone.

want to restrict sexually explicit books because of the proliferation of erotica), and music.

FILTERS ON GOOGLE CHROME

Again, very impressed by Google. The two options you should choose from depending on your kid's maturity are either "Try to Block Mature Sites" or "Only Allow Certain Sites." We really like the "Only Allow Certain Sites" option because you can approve requests from your kid for certain sites. This keeps you in the loop, keeps the conversation going, and is easy. Both of these allow you to additionally "Manage Sites" which allows you to "Approve" or "Block" any site. This is helpful for sites that are harmful or even just distracting. There are parents we know who have "Blocked" gmail.com and facebook.com from themselves just because they were distracting. That parent might be writing the sentence you are reading right now.

FILTERS ON GOOGLE SEARCH

This gives you the power to force Safe Search to be on. You should definitely do this. However, know that you can't ***depend*** on this. We'd recommend an outside filtering and monitoring app like Covenant Eyes when you are ready to give more internet freedom to your kid.

APPS FOR GOOGLE ASSISTANT

This is up to you. Should you ever need to restrict the apps allowed by Google Assistant, this is where you would do so.

ANDROID APPS

Okay, here we go. It is imperative to know what each app does and ask, "What is it for?" Apps are amazing. Apps can be distracting. Apps can directly or indirectly lead straight to porn and the horrors of the Dark Web, and everything else we discussed in this chapter. You need to use your discretion to determine what is safe, and what your kid is ready for. This category will show all apps on the phone, both allowed and blocked. To change these settings, select the app and toggle the "Allowed" switch. You can also customize the specific tools each app may use in the "Permissions" section within each app's tab.

LOCATION

Yes, you want to see your kid's location. Not only does this feel great, it keeps you from nagging them and always asking, "Where are you?" Be sure to set this functionality up!

SETTINGS

Lastly, you can change all these settings and more in the "Settings" tab for your kid's phone in Family Link. Find their phone on their Family Link page and choose "Settings." (NOTE: You can also make the phone play a sound if it is lost.) Most of these settings you have already customized, or are already pre-loaded with the choices you would want. For example, it is pre-set that your kid cannot download apps from unknown sources. Also notice that you can change your kid's phone passcode here, if need be.

22. Texting & Social Media

Technology is a useful servant but a dangerous master.

— Christian Lange, Nobel Peace Prize Recipient

Blessed is the one
who walks not in ***the counsel of the wicked,***
nor stands in the way of sinners,
nor sits in the seat of scoffers;
but their delight is in the law of the Lord,
and on his law he meditates day and night.
They are like a tree
planted by streams of water
that yields its fruit in its season,
and its leaf does not wither.
In all that they do, they prosper.

— Psalm 1:1- 3, Emphasis Added

It's time to learn how to setup your kid's smartphone for success in relation to texting and social media.

Let's start with a thought experiment: Imagine your child, whom you dearly love, is struggling deeply. So, you hire a counselor, someone with a large base of knowledge to give them advice. At first, things seem to be going well, but it is hard to tell. It takes you a few months before you notice signs of dysfunction in your child's behavior.

After counseling sessions, your kid is unwilling to tell you what their counselor is telling them and for some reason your kid wants to start inviting the counselor over for dinner. Actually, your kid wants to spend a few hours every day with them. A clinical therapist would draw the line somewhere. This counselor hasn't.

Now imagine one day you are able to overhear the counseling session and you overhear ***wicked*** counsel. Your son struggles with bulimia and the counselor is teaching him ways to lose more weight without you knowing. Or your daughter struggles with her body image and the counselor is body shaming her and telling her she is worthless.

So what do you do? You kick down the door, pull your child out of the counseling clinic, and burn down the building with the counselor inside![61]

Ok, maybe you are not *that* extreme. But in this scenario, I would certainly be tempted to let the wicked counselor know how I felt. Let's end the thought experiment with the obvious punchline: In many ways texting and social media are the voices of counselors, and our kid's phone is a small therapy office. The advice coming from those channels can be brilliant, but it is often ***wicked***. In light of that, let's review some of the dangers and best practices surrounding texting and social media.

DOMAIN 7: TEXTING DANGERS

INTERRUPTIONS

50,000,000,000 messages are exchanged every day worldwide. They have a 99% open rate. Adults 18 to 24 years old send and receive over 128 texts every day. Adults 45 to 54 send and receive 33 texts a day. We know this is true because we read it on the internet. (And Twilio and Experian Marketing Services did some studies.) How many things do we let our "99% open-rate" texts interrupt?

PRESSURE

Students tell us all the time that they have consistent pressure to maintain their text messages when they receive texts at night *and especially when they receive any texts from their mom!* Many actually like going to camp and being phone free, (well at least after the first 24 hour detox!) because they don't have to maintain the expectation to return texts while there.

TEXTING JUXTAPOSITIONS

Is texting what it seems to be? Texting is private because there is no

[61] Too far? Yeah, you're right. Way too far.

accountability. Texting is public because everything can be recorded, and sent to everyone. Texting is personal because it is one-to-one communication. Texting is impersonal because there is no tone, eye contact, body language, or touch (but there are emojis, and those are awesome). Texting feels secure because there is less risk of rejection. Texting is cowardly because you say things you would never say in person. We don't think about it much, but we should know what texting *is*, and what it *isn't*.

BULLYING

We all know bullying is a problem that technology has exacerbated, so much so that it has gained the term "cyberbullying." A comedian insightfully spoke about this on CONAN. He joked that kids need to try out being mean to see what it's like. Saying, "You're fat!" to someone's face elicits pain on the face of the accused. The kid sees this, and thinks, *"That felt bad."* But when a kid types, "You're fat," on social media, they are not met with the pained person's face. It is far easier to say that was fun and try it again when you are distanced from the person you are hurting. This is just the beginning of issue with cyberbullying, but you get the danger here.

SEXTING

What may surprise you is that sexting has become a normal part of dating. If you have a daughter, there's a good chance she will be solicited for nude pictures. If you have a son, there is a good chance he will be sent nudes that he never asked for. Or even vice versa in both of these situations. What really shocked us is that many girls who are not asked for nudes want boys to ask them. Ultimately, they want to be wanted, and this is how culture is telling them to measure their value. Encourage your kid to never send

> *I wish boys would ask me for nude photos.*
>
> *~Jamie, 8th Grade*

suggestive pictures of themselves, to never pass along suggestive images, and to tell you immediately when they receive them. Let them know that they can blame you in order to scare their friends into not sending them nudes. More on this later . . .

DELETING STUFF

Any transgressions that your kid might not want you to see can be hidden by erasing it. A whole text message conversation can be deleted, or individual texts can be deleted, and you would never know.

EMOJI SLANG AND GENERAL SLANG

There are entire dictionaries online for emoji sexual slang. Check out Axis' Parent Guide on Teen Slang[62] at axis.org/guides for an in-depth look at current teen slang.

TEXTING BEST PRACTICES

The big picture behind texting is visibility. I remember speaking at an Axis event and one of our great team members had just broken up with her boyfriend. Unbeknownst to me, this unhappy ex-boyfriend was calling her a bitch[63] and other terrible things via text. I had no idea. And she was silently bearing this abuse. Texting creates an entire universe of privacy and vulnerability that has never existed before.

We have just one best practice for you: monitoring. One of the best ways to protect your kid and help them mature is to tastefully monitor their texts, or just let them know you have a copy of the texts. This will scare them because we live in a world that worships privacy. But remember, we are better in community than in private. If you are doing nothing wrong, then there is no reason to fear the authorities in your life. The authorities should actually commend you for your good actions. How to monitor? Wait for the Phone Setup Guide at the end.

DOMAIN 8: SOCIAL MEDIA DANGERS

There are many great things about social media . . . but it's not our goal in this section to talk about those! Here are some things that can be

[62] It's funny. It's terrifying.
[63] Sorry for the distasteful language but the story is real.

used for evil. Yikes!

INSTAGRAM

Everyone looks perfect so it creates a culture of comparison, anxiety, and fear of missing out. #FOMO. There are a lot of photos of people in their skimpy underwear, too.

YOUTUBE

It feels like every video thumbnail has a woman in a bikini advertising that video. Trolling (a form of cyberbullying) is out of control in the comments section. You can find videos that support any belief you want. #flatearth. Autoplay can waste a fair amount of time and it can autoplay you into videos that are *very* questionable. YouTube stars/ influencers can normalize wrong beliefs or behaviors all to make a little cash.[64] There is soft-core porn on YouTube, especially in popular music videos. And, lastly, if you post videos (especially if you are young) predators can reach out to you.

TUMBLR

Tumblr used to be known for tons of pornographic posts and links to pornographic videos. Recently it was purchased by Automattic, who claims that they will ban pornographic and sexually graphic content on the site. This might make it safer for your kid than other sites. However, there are still affinity groups that can support any belief you want to have. Tumblr also has lower privacy settings than most social media platforms, meaning your teen is more exposed to potential unwanted advances. Pros and cons . . .

TWITTER

Some porn—buyer beware. Comments and roasting can be toxic at times. Cyberbullying is the big one here. And subtweets.[65]

---

64 Like this behavior: axis.org/sanity-subway. Licking a NYC subway handrail. What folks will do for a buck.

65 A subtweet is a tweet that mentions another person on Twitter without actually tagging them in the message, therefore that user is not notified and usually won't find out.

FACEBOOK

Your grandma is going to comment on every post you make.
Many kids use Facebook only for their family these days, but all joking aside, it poses the exact same threats as any other social media.

WHATSAPP, KIK, FACEBOOK MESSENGER

These all have the same challenges as texting.

SNAPCHAT

Snapchat is full of threats. With disappearing snaps, a culture of sexting, and a very sexually graphic stories section, we'd be remiss if we didn't mention this teen favorite in more detail. There's nothing quite like Snapchat.

- ***It's a Brilliant App.*** Where other social media platforms started on computers (Exhibit A: Facebook), Snapchat has been a mobile-only experience from the beginning. The only way to truly appreciate it is to use it yourself. This may be overwhelming at first—similar to learning a new language—so just ask the nearest teen for a tour of how it works. What you'll discover first are its augmented reality "filters" for selfies, which are fun, colorful, a bit silly, and constantly changing. You've gotta admit it though—they're fun!
- ***Disappearing Snaps.*** Second, you'll experience what Snapchat is best known for: the disappearing Snap (a photo that disappears immediately upon viewing). This impermanence creates intrigue and scarcity while allowing users to be in the moment and not worry about how they look . You can see how this would be appealing in contrast to Instagram's focus on the perfect shot and edited perfection. But as you can imagine, the disappearing nature has encouraged many to use Snapchat to "sext" without fear of being seen by the wrong eyes . . . but, as any teen can tell you, images can always be captured via screenshot and distributed to others in a matter of seconds. The app does not prevent screenshots; it only notifies the sender that a screenshot was taken.

- ***Oh, the Snapstreak.*** Third, you'll behold the Snapstreak, a record of how many days in a row two users have snapped each other. These Snapstreaks are so addictive that some users have streaks in the *thousands*. So if you want to start World War III in your home, simply threaten to take away your kid's phone access for 24 hours so that all their Snapstreaks end. (They'll be furious, but don't worry; they'll find a creative way to keep their Snapstreaks going behind your back like borrowing their friend's phone, logging into their personal Snap account, and sending the necessary Snaps.)
- ***Stories.*** Fourth, you'll come across another one of Snapchat's inventions: Stories, i.e., a set of photos and/or videos that can be made public and are only viewable for 24 hours. They feel authentic/personal and are quite often unfiltered. Anyone can post a story, but what makes them especially interesting is how you can follow celebrities' personal lives through their stories.
- ***Discover.*** Finally, you'll unearth the Discover section, which features articles, videos, and short TV shows from major brands (intermixed with celebs' Stories). Sadly, unless some miracle has changed the popular culture overnight, a great word to describe much of the content in the Discover section is "smutty."
- ***Other Stuff.*** Oh, and finally, *finally,* there are Snapmaps, Snapcash, Emoji codes, and many other features. Check out our Parent's Guide to Snapchat[66] for more! Whew.

SOCIAL MEDIA BEST PRACTICES

Now that you've taken a crash course in the dangers that can come from social media, let's take a look at some of the best things you can do to protect your kid (and yourself)!

---

[66] Again, the Parent's Guide to Snapchat is free with *Smartphone Sanity* at axis.org/sanity-snapchat.

NOTHING IS PERFECT

Own this Fact. There is NO perfect solution other than you. Everything is built on trust and your relationship with your wonderful kid. There are some great monitoring solutions BUT nothing is perfect and nothing will replace your relationship with your kid.

KNOW ALL THEIR APPS

As always, know all the apps on your kid's phone. Be especially vigilant with social media apps. *ESPECIALLY* the social media apps hidden a few folders deep!

USERNAMES AND PASSWORDS

And, just like with the rest of the phone, know all usernames and passwords for all social media apps.

ONE SOCIAL MEDIA AT A TIME

When you get your kid a phone we would encourage you not to let them have social media immediately. And when you do decide to start that journey, only let them have one version of social media at first. Plan on journeying with them as they learn about using this social media.

BEWARE OF MULTIPLE ACCOUNTS

A "Finsta" is teen slang for Fake Instagram. Many teens have multiple accounts on social media platforms. One account is the main account for their grandma to follow. The other accounts are for their inner circle of friends. The monitoring software we will recommend will help you find out if they have other accounts, but again, it is not perfect. One idea is to let them have multiple accounts and just stay in conversation about them.

DIRECT MESSAGES

Many social media apps have direct/private messaging. This is something you should check frequently because these direct messages have very similar dangers as texting. For example we know of teens who were caught sexting by using the DM capabilities of Pinterest! Seriously? Seriously.

LEARN APP ETIQUETTE FROM THEM

There are many unwritten rules about each type of social media. Make sure you let your kid teach you about them.

GROWING IN WISDOM FROM YOU

On the flip-side, there are many unwritten rules about human nature. Make sure you teach your kid about them by helping them grow into healthy social media use. Here's how:

- *Permission to Post.* Before they post they should get permission from you. You should review it and make sure everything is okay. There are so many ways to hurt their friends' feelings inadvertently. This is a great chance to teach **respect and empathy**. Over time you will trust them to post with wisdom.
- *Know Who They Are Following.* Should they follow someone that they are not friends with in real life? What about celebrity accounts? What about strangers?
- *Follow Their Accounts, But Don't be Invasive.* Follow their account and periodically check it. On the whole don't comment on or participate with it; but, it is good for them to know you have some oversight on their account.

WANT TO LIVE IN THE 1950S?

Whoa, there! Hold your horses. We know all this information about texting and social media is scary and possibly even infuriating. That righteous anger toward evil is good, but the answer is not to remove technology and pretend it does not exist. Remember the wicked counselor? You cannot shield your kid from it by taking away their phone forever. What you *can* do is become that voice of counsel in their ear. This chapter's experience will help you create a safe space for them to talk to you about what the wicked counselor has to offer. And don't forget to check out the Phone Setup Guide on Mirroring and Monitoring!

EXPERIENCE: CREATE AN OPEN ATMOSPHERE, PICK 1

You want your son or daughter to be open with you and make the right decisions when it comes to texting and social media. However, it's not always easy to talk about these things with them. Look over the following list of attitudes and actions to create an atmosphere where you can talk about the dangers of texting and social media freely. Which one of these resonates the most with you? Tell a friend or spouse, or journal about it today!

ONE: IT'S *GOD'S* PHONE AND *YOU*, THEIR PARENT, ARE THE STEWARD.

Therefore, you can have access to it to check it whenever you would like because you love them and want to protect them. *And* you can setup mirroring and/or monitoring. Food for thought: *Would you be willing to give someone access your phone at anytime to check on you?*

TWO: THE RIGHTEOUS HAVE NOTHING TO HIDE

"For rulers hold no terror for those who do right, but for those who do wrong. Do you want to be free from fear of the one in authority? Then do what is right and you will be commended" (Romans 13:3). If they have nothing to hide, you'll trust them, get bored, and not check their phone as much. Everyone wins. *Do you model an openness with your phone because you have nothing to hide?*

THREE: DON'T BE A CREEP

Texting is still pretty intimate, and if you check everything and then pick on them about it, they will not like you. Choose your battles. *When you review their phone are you kind or controlling?*

> "*When you review their phone, are you kind or controlling?*"

FOUR: BE SEEN

There is something about knowing that someone who loves you is checking your texts. It has a way of keeping us honest. Not to be too extreme, but there is a reason that church nurseries have windows. *Do you have visibility with your online actions?*

FIVE: BE THE SCAPEGOAT

Let them know that if you see something bad on their phone that you will tell their friend who sent it and that friend's parents. If they know this clearly, they will warn their friends NOT to send them inappropriate content. See what we did there? Still, be sensitive with this. *Are you safe enough that your kid can depend on you as a moral backstop in hard situations?*

SIX: TEXT THEM!

Sometimes it may be awkward to start some conversations face to face. Don't be afraid to start it via text or their favorite messaging app and then finish it face to face. I know it may feel cowardly, but sometimes this is a great way to speak your kid's language. *Have you tried to have fun, even whimsical, conversations with your kid via their messaging app of choice?*[67]

[67] A pastor in the Midwest had a very strained relationship with his daughter. She left for college and refused to answer his calls so he humbled himself and reached out to her via text. It slowly got the conversation going so that in a few weeks he was able to ask her for forgiveness and restore their relationship.

Phone Setup Guide!
Phone Mirroring & Monitoring

It may be true that integrity is doing the right thing when no one is watching; however, it certainly helps me do the right thing when I ***know*** someone else is watching. Until your kid gets to the point where they can do the right thing by themselves, mirroring and monitoring can help you guide them to that habit. The fact that you *can* see their texts, should you choose to, will go a long way.

Mirroring is the ability to setup a parallel device and link it to your kid's phone in order to see all the text messages sent from their phone. Monitoring, on the other hand, is a paid service that reads, records, and reports on your kid's messaging.

Thanks to Apple's Screen Time and Google's Family Link, your kid doesn't have to have texting allowed on their phone. We recommend limiting texting or excluding it especially when they get their first phone. Below are the keys to the kingdom. Find the sections appropriate to your devices.

iPhone & Android: Phone Setup Guide Mirroring Your Kid's Phone

APPLE: COMPUTER MIRRORING

If your kid has an iPhone and you have an Apple computer you can set up a new user on your Apple computer, login to messages under that user account and use your kid's Apple ID. This will put a mirror copy of every text onto that account after you login each time. Do NOT sync with iCloud. If you do every time they delete a text on their phone it will be deleted on your computer. When you initially set this up, if you do sync with iCloud, past text messages will be downloaded to your computer. If you don't, only future texts will be added. Once you do the initial sync with iCloud, in preferences select stop syncing with iCloud. NOTE: We have found this method to be finicky. But it's free! If you are computer savvy, give it a try!

APPLE: OTHER DEVICE MIRRORING

If you have an iPad that you don't want your messages stored on, you can link it to your kid's Apple ID and have a mirrored copy of all texts on that iPad. Keep in mind not to send personal text messages from that iPad because it will look like they were sent from your kid.

APPLE: MIRRORING IPHONE MESSAGES ON YOUR ANDROID PHONE

As of the printing of this book, this doesn't work. Sorry.

ANDROID: COMPUTER, IPHONE, TABLET MIRRORING

Find the Messages+ App in the Apple App Store, Mac App Store, or on your other computer or tablet in the Google Play Store. Download it and add your kid's phone number. Once installed, you will have access to all their future texts; however, if they delete a text it will be synced across all devices.

iPhone & Android: Phone Setup Guide Monitoring Your Kid's Phone

Monitoring is especially important in regard to texting. Texting in particular is easy to hide because you can delete individual sensitive texts or entire conversations. Parents already have a full-time job and they don't need another job reading their kids texts!

Also, sexting is a cultural phenomenon that is out of control. Sexual-exploitation and child-pornography laws can come into play so great care is needed in the handling of sexting cases involving people under 18. Needless to say, monitoring can make great leaps in controlling the unwieldy-world of sexting. And sexting situations can get stressful and blurry very quickly. In our experience, most parents refuse to believe their child would ever send a sext of themselves, so it is important to have evidence when informing other parents. Here are a few ways you can monitor your kid's phone.

MANUAL CHECK

Pick up their phone every now and then and manually check their messages. Manually login to their social accounts and look around. Don't be afraid to trust the Holy Spirit to prompt you. If you sense something just check their phone.

MANUAL MONITORING

TeenSafe.com or uKnowKids.com - $15/month

Have a record of all sent, received, and deleted texts. It can also scan for hidden social media accounts, allowing you to monitor Facebook, Twitter, Instagram, WhatsApp, and more.

ARTIFICIAL INTELLIGENCE MACHINE MONITORING

Bark.us - $9/month

Highly recommended! Bark proactively monitors text messages, emails, and 24+ different social networks for potential safety concerns, so busy parents can save time and gain peace of mind. You will NOT have a record of all sent, received, and deleted texts. Instead, Bark will review almost all interactions and then send you notifications whenever it recognizes something high risk. Bark will save you time and allow your kid to have "privacy" in non-dangerous issues. Pretty cool.

REMOVING TEXTING/SOCIAL MEDIA OR PAUSING IT

On iPhone you can shut off or pause any app,[68] including Messages. For Android use the all-powerful Family Link.

---

[68] Well, you can't shut off the ability to make a phone call, or the settings app. But let's be honest. That's not why your kid wants a phone.

“

Your kid will always have access to an unfiltered, unmonitored, & unrestricted phone.

”

23. Their Friend's Phone

> *I wake up in cold sweats every so often thinking, what did we bring to the world?*
>
> — Tony Fadell, Co-inventor of iPhone, Creator of Nest

> *The eyes of the Lord are in every place, keeping watch on the evil and the good.*
>
> — Proverbs 15:3

We've covered a lot of scary stuff this step, everything from sneaks your kid may use to the wicked counsel that can happen via texting or social media. By this point, you may want to smash your kid's phone with a hammer.[69]

As much as you may be tempted to throw in the towel and curb-smash your kid's phone, this is not how *you* parent. You are wise, loving, and committed to your kid's well-being. You have a Growth Mindset and a deep experience with the gospel that informs your appreciation of technology. And . . . you have a plan for your family's technology (or at least you will soon!) that gives you confidence and a pathway to success, so you don't need to go Thor on your kid's phone.

Yet, there is one more thing to mention. With all the work you have done there is still one big challenge that is outside of your control. With all of your clear communication and intentional tools in place, your kid will always have access to an unfiltered, unmonitored, and unrestricted

---

69 . . . like the parents in this video: axis.org/sanity-smash. Watch it, it's cheaper than therapy. Or watch as much as you can stand. (It might even be instructive to watch it with your kids, but you should watch it first by yourself because the video is definitely PG-13.) These are parents who have had *enough*. It's really sad. It's really intense. And it's *not* you.

phone. "HOW!?" you ask. "I've constructed a virtual Fort Knox!" Well, unfortunately, their friends will have phones and they will show your kid things on it or send your kid things from it that you would never wish them to see.

Another mom noticed her sons countenance had fallen. She gently asked him what was on his mind and he started crying. One of his friends had shown him a video of a man murdering a box full of puppies with a hammer. Her son could not unsee this and he was clearly disturbed.[70] This is a spiritual battle, and the enemy *is looking for your kid.* So what do you do?

- Consistently reaffirm to your kid: "You can tell me anything, I'll be fair, and I won't overreact."
- Ask them kindly if they have seen anything inappropriate.
- Give them a game plan of what to do if they are shown or sent something inappropriate. Consider role playing what to do. Have different plans of action for porn, sexting, violence, suicidal threats, bullying, etc.
- Be the scapegoat. They can tell their friends not to send them anything because you monitor their phone. This helps them save face (unfortunately, it's come to that).
- The most important thing is to give your kids a heads-up so they are not blindsided. Yes, this could mean having a conversation with them earlier than you wish you had to have that conversation. Remember the axiom from Craig Gross, founder of porn prevention website XXXChurch: "What you talk about with your kids they will talk about with you."

> *What you talk about with your kid, they will talk about with you.*
>
> ~ Craig Gross

[70] I hear these stories when I travel and teach about smartphones. I never cease to be heart-broken over the stories I hear.

When you give them fair warning it gives them permission to come to you if—no—***when*** something happens.

- Give them a game plan on what to do if they accidentally see something on their phone that they didn't expect. Let them know they can tell you.
- Let them know you'll be safe and you will not shame them. Seeing something extreme and evil will make them feel shame and will make them want to hide from you. Kill that shame with empathy. Don't let it stay secret, silent, or judged.
- If they are shown something sexual it could cause them to be aroused. You want them to process that with you or a counselor! You don't want arousal to be fused with shame.

And, remind them that even if you can't see, monitor, or filter something, God sees. "The eyes of the Lord are in every place, keeping watch on the evil and the good" (Proverbs 15:3). God is a loving father and he disciplines those He loves. Not in a vindictive way, but in a kind way that leads to repentance and therefore life! The kindness of God leads to repentance, not the other way around. A heart connection with your kid is the ***only*** Fort Knox you can rely on. Give them love, acceptance, and confidence that you are a safe confidant.

EXPERIENCE: OPEN THE DOOR TO CONVERSATION

Once you create an environment in which your kid can ask you anything, talking with them about these hard issues will be much more comfortable. To make this space, open the door to tough conversations by talking about something *not about them*. This experience is to ask your kid if any of their friends have ever seen something on a phone that your kid deemed inappropriate.

Make it NOT about them, but their friend. Ask them if it made them uncomfortable, and if the friend did anything about it. This can be anything from bullying to violence to sexting. Whatever they talk about with you is a good start. The rest will follow. Consider starting this conversation via text.

24. Success Stories! And Social Media Case Study!

Just one step left! Great job! We aren't done, *but we are so close*. We understand that you have been hit with a lot of technical info, a lot of shocking things the phone can do, and a lot of reading. Do not despair! You are not alone. Many have read this book before you. Here are some of their stories.

> *I simply cannot articulate how deeply grateful I am for all the information I am learning and how your group has directed us to frame all of this in the context of relationship with our kids. I marvel again (why am I continually taken aback?) at God's perfect timing in orchestrating this 'course' for this stage in my parenting—not a moment too soon, but neither a moment too late. I sat and cried tears of gratitude this morning as I read the information I have known I need, but have been at a loss as to where to find. Today I prayed God's rich blessings on Axis as an organization and on each of you as individuals. Your work is for such a time as this.*
>
> *Wowza! This is fantastic and clear information.*
>
> *Learning how to use my phone and my kids' is so awesome. There are so many things I never learned about on my devices and now I am finally way more educated. It feels really good to not be in the dark about it. I have felt like I was too old or too behind the times to get this stuff but it's just a matter of having someone like you lay it out step by step in a Christian worldview.*

Please keep sharing your feedback with us at axis.org!

EXPERIENCE: CONVERSATION KIT ON SOCIAL MEDIA

Below are five different Conversation Kits on different cultural challenges, accelerated by the smartphone, that your kid may face. They are fun videos designed with your kid in mind are about 45 minutes each. We are including a free video Conversation Kit on Social Media or you could choose to spend a few bucks and buy a different one.

Free video Conversation Kit Included with This Book:
Conversation Kit on Social Media[71]

Other Conversation Kits for Sale at Axis.org/Guides:
Conversation Kit on Relationships
Conversation Kit on Identity
Conversation Kit on Gender
Conversation Kit on Anxiety

[71] Experience this great product at axis.org/sanity-social. I hate to be so partial, but I love our Conversation Kit on Social Media. **It's my favorite.** The "toast puppies" video three minutes in—you'll know it when you see it—is hilarious. And overall it is a win if you watch it with your kid. It's not condemning and gets the conversation going. We know . . . this is a book, not a video. But we wanted to give you our best stuff. Feel free to skip and come back at another time!

25. Activity 3: Hang Out with Your Friends

This is a fun chance to enter into your story with some parents like you. Are you ready? We want you to share your smartphone story in the first part of this activity! Here are two tips for sharing your story in an impactful way:

- Practice sharing the context of your story in addition to the content. Share how you felt, what was going through your mind, and how the event impacted you in addition to the "who and where" kind of details. Listen for these kinds of details in others' stories too.
- It's also important to practice awareness, curiosity, and kindness when listening to others share their stories. ***Awareness*** allows us to focus on the storyteller and how he or she feels. ***Curiosity*** allows us to ask good questions to create deeper connection. ***Kindness*** helps shape our stories and how we hear others' stories.[72] Practice these as you share stories with other parents.

EXPERIENCE: HANG OUT WITH YOUR FRIENDS

Here are the details for Activity 3, which involves sharing your story with other parents. If you haven't yet done so, put a one hour dessert on your family's calendar. As always, there are three options for this experience. Do whichever you have time for!

1. Look, I'm Busy

---

72 Check out Restoration Project, an amazing ministry for men to fully engage as fathers, husbands, and brothers. We've learned so much from them about Experience, Story, and Blessing, as well as Awareness, Curiosity, and Kindness.

2. You Can Do It!
3. The Overachiever Edition

WHAT'S THE ACTIVITY?

Experience: Share a dessert and/or an appropriate beverage with the parents of another family.
Story: Share about what you are learning and ask them about their smartphone best practices.
Blessing: Pray together for guidance and wisdom.

Here's How It Works: You (the parents) invite other parents to join you in **experience** and **story** by doing a simple dessert together (either go out for ice cream or invite them to your place for dessert, wine, coffee, or something nice). The goal during this time is to have an intentional conversation **with a peer** where you practice sharing your story and entering into theirs. This is meant as an experience for the parents only. The goal of this time is for you to practice sharing and hearing the stories of others "in a similar boat" as you. It's a chance to connect on a deeper level around your smartphone story. Community is hugely important when striving to use your smartphones in a better way.

OPTION 1: LOOK, I'M BUSY.

Step 1 and Done: Invite one of your favorite couples or a friend over who is a true peer. Tell them what you have learned. No kids.

OPTION 2: YOU CAN DO IT!

Step 1: *Plan a 1-2 hour window in your calendar* where you share dessert or something similar with a "parental unit" in a similar life stage as you, and discuss your journey with your smartphones. This experience is intended for you and another couple (not kids).

Step 2: *Invite the other parents.* Use the email template at the end of this section to invite a couple or parent(s) you wish to talk to about smartphones. **If possible email/text them before the end of the day.** The email template is intended to give them a little head's up on what you're doing with *Smartphone Sanity* so they know what to expect from the evening. **Tip:** Invite folks until you get a "yes." If the first option turns you down, go to option two. Trust God to have the right "parental unit" say yes. Don't let one "I'm not available" make you put off trying this experience with another family.

Step 3: *Plan the dessert.* Pick something easy and casual here. It doesn't have to be dessert. It could be coffee or a bottle of wine. But, this isn't about what you eat as much as it is "stepping out there" and inviting another family/parental unit into your smartphone experience. This will be good for you and good for them. It's a great opportunity to simply have an excuse to connect on a deeper level about something that probably matters to each of you.

Step 4: *Prepare for the Conversation.* The email template will give your invitee(s) a heads up that you want to talk about smartphones. Prepare your own story to tell, and just go from there. You can share what you've learned, how you're growing, what problems you've encountered, or anything that you want or need to talk about. Some parents have chosen to share big points from their *Smartphone Sanity* experience. The point is to support each other and share ideas. You are not alone, and neither are they! Hopefully you can bond and brainstorm with your guests through these conversation prompts.

Step 5: *Enjoy dessert and enter into each other's stories.* You should lead the way in the conversation, as your guests haven't thought about their phones nearly as much as you recently and our phone activity can feel like a very intimate thing at times. If you lead the way with your stories, that should open up your friends to share theirs.

Step 6: *If you are comfortable, pray together.* This is the blessing part of the experience. A simple prayer at the end is great! This *is* a spiritual battle, and we have the ultimate victory on our side. Never forget that.

OPTION 3: OVERACHIEVER EDITION

There's two optional activities that can include the kids, but the intentional conversation should be between just the adults. If you can make it happen, this extended option allows the kids to enjoy each other's company as well as the parents to talk in private.

Steps 1-6: Same instructions as Option 2. **Additionally,** either before or after your dessert discussion, do one of the following activities with the whole family:

- Watch a current movie that deals with technology and discuss the issues related to smartphones from the movie.
- Do something interactive and fun with your phones that you'd normally never do, like a group video game or something similar. This is a good way to connect both digitally and physically, and a great opportunity for reflection on our phones. Ask your kids for advice on what digital activity they would enjoy the most. Let them be your tour guide and just enjoy the experience! If a good teachable moment comes up for you and the kids, great. If not, that's okay too.

EMAIL INVITATION TEMPLATE: [73]

Recently I've invested in a book called *Smartphone Sanity* to help our family think through how we use our smartphones, and particularly to help our kids use them well.

One of our activities is to invite other parents over for dessert and to share in an intentional conversation around each other's smartphone stories.

If you're able to make it, we'd like to ask you if you could give a couple of thoughts to some questions we want to think about to make our time more meaningful.

Your Signature

RESPONSE EMAIL TEMPLATE (AFTER THEY CONFIRM):

Hey ________,

That's awesome! We're excited to spend some time with you.

To prepare for the conversation, could you think of a story about how your smartphone has impacted your life recently, for better or worse? Also think of one of the biggest smartphone challenges you have faced with your

73 Isn't copy and paste great? Axis.org/sanity-email2.

kids and one of your biggest successes! We're excited to talk about these things with you, as we have been thinking about them a lot lately.

If you can't get to it, that's okay—if you don't get to it before we meet I guarantee you'll still have ideas to bring to the table.

See you soon!
Your Signature

STEP 4

make a plan

make a plan

26. Essential Conversation 4: You Can Tell Me Anything!

You have made it to the final stretch of *Smartphone Sanity*. We hope you've loved your time learning about the smartphone, but that you have loved even more learning how to connect with the heart of your child.

Step Four is about applying all we've learned in the past three steps and turning it into a Family Phone Agreement. This agreement will produce short-term success while leading your kid into realizing long-term character goals for their life. Get excited! Each chapter in this part will focus on a different aspect of the Family Phone Agreement, the short-term solution for your family's phones. The Family Phone Agreement is a contract you will write with your kids to agree on how your family will use your phones. You'll build this agreement together as a whole family at your first Family Phone Agreement Meeting after finishing this book (instructions will follow).

You already know that we start each step by soaking in the scriptural foundation for one of Axis' Four Essential Smartphone Conversations. This conversation is about the solution that lasts long after the Family Phone Agreement is over.

Conversation 1:	Very Good, Cursed, & Redeemed.
Conversation 2:	What Is It For?
Conversation 3:	We are on a Journey of Trust with a Destination of Independence.
Conversation 4:	**You Can Tell Me Anything!**

The fourth Essential Conversation is about building a strong heart connection with your kids so that they are always comfortable enough to tell you anything. So, as always, let's dive into scripture, looking at perhaps the most famous parable in Scripture, the parable of the prodigal son from Luke 15. In this parable we can see Jesus showing us God's heart. Pay special attention to how the father is able to handle and absorb the harsh things his sons tell him.

> *And he [Jesus] said, "There was a man who had two sons. And the younger of them said to his father, 'Father, give me the share of property that is coming to me.' And he divided his property between them. Not many days later, the younger son gathered all he had and took a journey into a far country, and there he squandered his property in reckless living. And when he had spent everything, a severe famine arose in that country, and he began to be in need. So he went and hired himself out to one of the citizens of that country, who sent him into his fields to feed pigs. And he was longing to be fed with the pods that the pigs ate, and no one gave him anything.*
>
> *"But when he came to himself, he said, 'How many of my father's hired servants have more than enough bread, but I perish here with hunger! I will arise and go to my father, and I will say to him, "Father, I have sinned against heaven and before you. I am no longer worthy to be called your son. Treat me as one of your hired servants."' And he arose and came to his father. But while he was still a long way off, his father saw him and felt compassion, and ran and embraced him and kissed him. And the son said to him, 'Father, I have sinned against heaven and before you. I am no longer worthy to be called your son.' But the father said to his servants, 'Bring quickly the best robe, and put it on him, and put a ring on his hand, and shoes on his feet. And bring the fattened calf and kill it, and let us eat and celebrate. For this my son was dead, and is alive again; he was lost, and is found.' And they began to celebrate.*
>
> *"Now his older son was in the field, and as he came and drew near to the house, he heard music and dancing. And he called one of the servants and asked what these things meant. And he said to him, 'Your brother has come, and your father has killed the fattened calf, because he has received him back safe and sound.' But he was angry and refused to go in. His father came out and entreated him, but he answered his father, 'Look, these many*

years I have served you, and I never disobeyed your command, yet you never gave me a young goat, that I might celebrate with my friends. But when this son of yours came, who has devoured your property with prostitutes, you killed the fattened calf for him!' And he said to him, 'Son, you are always with me, and all that is mine is yours. It was fitting to celebrate and be glad, for this your brother was dead, and is alive; he was lost, and is found.'"

— Luke 15:11–32

We all know this story and you've probably heard it taught in Sunday school and sermons. But let's take a quick glance at the context leading up to the Parable of the Prodigal Son:

Now the tax collectors and sinners were all drawing near to hear him [Jesus]. And the Pharisees and the scribes grumbled, saying, "This man receives sinners and eats with them."

So he told them this parable: "What man of you, having a hundred sheep, if he has lost one of them, does not leave the ninety-nine in the open country, and go after the one that is lost, until he finds it? And when he has found it, he lays it on his shoulders, rejoicing. And when he comes home, he calls together his friends and his neighbors, saying to them, 'Rejoice with me, for I have found my sheep that was lost.' Just so, I tell you, there will be more joy in heaven over one sinner who repents than over ninety-nine righteous persons who need no repentance.

"Or what woman, having ten silver coins, if she loses one coin, does not light a lamp and sweep the house and seek diligently until she finds it? And when she has found it, she calls together her friends and neighbors, saying, 'Rejoice with me, for I have found the coin that I had lost.' Just so, I tell you, there is joy before the angels of God over one sinner who repents."

— Luke 15:1–10

So one out of a hundred sheep is lost, sought, and found. Then, one coin out of ten is lost, sought, and found. Lastly, we come to the sons. How many are lost? Who is the father seeking? Whom does he find? Well, let's go back and see the words shared between the father and his two sons.

His younger son basically said to him, "I wish you were dead, give me my inheritance now so I can leave." That's hard to hear as a parent! But the father granted his son the inheritance—he split his property and sacrificed his status and livelihood to do so.

He sees his younger son come back to him and rejoices, though he hears his son say, "I am not worthy to be called your son," confessing all his wrongs. Another hard thing to absorb. Still the father celebrates to have his son home, heralding his homecoming with a grand party. Surely all that his son did hurt him, but he still loves him and invites him in to the celebration inside.

Lastly, the father is verbally confronted by his older son. Met with indignation and entitlement, the father hears his first son complain of unfair treatment for fulfilling his filial duties. His older son is so angry he does not even want to celebrate the return of his brother. What pain that must have inflicted on the father's heart. And yet the father invites his son to the party anyway.

If the father in Jesus' parable is God, we can see that God can handle all the hard things his children have to tell him, and to extend the parable, God can handle anything you have to tell him. He meets the younger son and the older son "in the field" and invites both of them to the party, just like he did with the tax collectors and the Pharisees who overheard his parable. God can handle our mess, he can handle whatever awful things we have to say to him, and he still wants us to be restored to him, and to join him at the party. Similarly, you can do the same for your kid. They need to hear you say, "You can tell me anything. Know that I'm rational, I'm loving, and I'm fair. I just want to invite you into the party!"

> *God invites us to the party!*

Yes, you and your kid are going to come across some tough things, but you can handle it because you are after their heart. So as you create your Family Phone Agreement to help navigate your family through the tough things, remember to foster trust by telling your kid, "You can tell me anything." Continue the *one conversation* and engage with your son or daughter's heart! Here's the ancient blessing, one final time:

> *The Lord bless you*
> *and keep you;*
> *the Lord make his face shine on you*
> *and be gracious to you;*
> *the Lord turn his face toward you*
> *and give you peace.*
>
> — Numbers 6:24–26

As you go into this fourth step, where you plan for success both now and in the long-run, may you demonstrate to your kid the loving heart of God.

They need to hear you say, "You can tell me anything." Remind them . . .

. . . that you are rational, loving, and fair. You just want to invite them into the party!

”

27. Under Authority: Parents & Privacy

Step Four is here! It is time to apply all you've learned. Starting now, you will start working on the Family Phone Agreement. What you will formulate is a living and dynamic document that will need to have changes made to it in the future as technology changes. This is not a vault to be sealed and locked, but a covenant that will grow as your family does!

The next five chapters will highlight different aspects of the agreement: Under Authority, Moral Compass, Self-Awareness, Self-Governance, and Community. These five concepts are the character you want your child to possess someday when they have full phone independence.

Don't worry! Along with content on each of those character traits we will also provide tactical, step-by-step actions for you to include in the agreement.

Each of these sections are very practical in the contract yet we decided to frame them philosophically, looking at the goals they aim at for your kid. Remember that **Journey of Trust with a Destination of Independence?** Each part focuses on an aspect of that independence, because this contract is only a stepping stone to your end-goal, not the be-all and end-all on the topic! This agreement is meant to provide guidelines and growth so that one day your kid *can* use their phone wisely *without* your supervision.

UNDER AUTHORITY

Your kid *has* to respect your authority as their parent now. They *have to respect* your rules about their phone, and they *have to respect* the agreement you will soon make with them because you are their authority right now. But what about down the road?

Even though they are currently under your authority, someday they will be on their own. BUT, that doesn't mean they will not be under another authority. It could be a boss, the government, an athletic league, or professional society. They will be under the spiritual authority of their church, and potentially they will be submitting their will to the needs of their wife or husband. In order to function (and flourish!), they will need to be able to live **under authority**. And, of course, you want them to realize and embrace that they will always be under God's authority. Being under God's authority means our phones are Very Good, Cursed, and can be Redeemed. Even if your kid owns their phone it is still true that God owns all phones. And since God can always see the things we wish to keep unseen, the idea of privacy is an illusion. Privacy can be complicated but we believe we must embrace two key ideas:

> *We are better in community than in isolation. We are only as sick as our secrets.*

- We are better in community than in isolation.
- There are no secrets; and, frankly, you are only as sick as your secrets.[74]

Thus, here is the part of the phone agreement on being **Under Authority:**

[74] I owe that phrase to a very intense mom who sat next to me on a plane. I was trying to prep a presentation I was giving the next day and she talked my *literal* face off. However, I am forever grateful. Also, she swears this phrase is from AA but I can't confirm that. If credit is due to AA, I gladly give it! My name is David, and you are only as sick as your secrets.

FAMILY PHONE AGREEMENT - PART 1 OF 4[75]

UNDER AUTHORITY: GOD

- Phones are Very Good, Cursed, & can be Redeemed.
- Since God owns everything, God owns all phones.

UNDER AUTHORITY: PARENTS

- As your parent, I am responsible to God as the ultimate steward of your phone when the phone is paid for by me and/or while you live in my home.
- You have no right to phone privacy.
- All passwords are accessible, including those for apps, and phones will be provided when asked for.
- We want to build your wisdom and restraint so one day you can be independent with your devices and not need oversight.

EXPERIENCE: MAD LIB ABOUT YOUR FAMILY

The mad-lib below will help you process this part of the contract in a fun way. Fill it out by yourself, and then again, with your kid! We are the ________________ Family. We love _________ and are really good at _________. We struggle with __________, and our biggest challenge is ____________. When it comes to our phones, we often __________, but we have a good habit of _________. We believe that phones are Very Good, Cursed, and can be Redeemed, and that God is the authority over them. Because of that, in our house privacy will look like ____________
____
____
_________________________________. As stewards of what God has given us, we will strive to use our phones for what they are for—God's glory.

75 For the full Agreement, and an editable link, skip a few pages ahead.

28. Moral Compass: Non-Negotiables

Throughout the first three steps of *Smartphone Sanity*, you no doubt have thought to yourself, "Just give me some rules!" Well, here we are, finally! The "non-negotiables" section of the Family Phone Agreement will focus on moral boundaries.

Don't get us wrong! We think your kid is a good kid; but, these things are better vocalized and agreed upon than left assumed. The non-negotiables are your prerogative as the adult in the home. Lay down the law, and teach your kid about developing a Moral Compass that loves what is good through these rules.

MORAL COMPASS

There are certain things that phones can do or be used for that are just *wrong*. While your kid might have an intuition for avoiding such things, without an agreement in place, they may just get sucked in by the larger culture.

> *"Some things are better vocalized and agreed upon than left assumed."*

In a world where anything goes and truth is relative, we must give our children tools to navigate the chaotic waters of culture. Perhaps the most important tool is their moral compass, something to tell them irrevocably whether what they are encountering is right or wrong.

When you lay out these non-negotiable rules, you declare that certain actions are wrong. The hope is that this example will help teach your kid to have their own moral compass to make decisions in the face of temptation and when new decisions come up in the future as technology evolves. Here are the non-negotiables we suggest:

- **Parents have full access**: Parents can ask for "your" phone at any time for any reason, and they will be able to because they know *all* passwords, *all* logins, and *all* apps on the phone. Parents will also be considerate and attempt to not exasperate their children.
- **No sneaky apps (intent on "hiding" or "secrets"):** There are apps that are intended to hide information and material. There are apps that subvert restrictions and "dig a tunnel under the wall" of protections that might be set up on the phone. These are not allowed.
- **Calls from parents are answered or responded to in an agreed upon time period:** This is a standard, base-level agreement that, if a parent calls, that call is NOT ignored, and any missed messages or calls are responded to within an agreed upon time limit that understands if the kid is in school, at home, etc.
- **GPS location services are always on:** These will be shared with the family so everyone knows where everyone is whenever they need.
- **No pornography and no sexting:** There are many damaging consequences to inappropriate material found on the internet. Porn hijacks the brain and is a drug that harms you, others, and the world. Sending nude pictures can create consequences that will last a lifetime. The internet is bigger and more powerful than any of us can appreciate. If your kid receives a sext they will notify you immediately.
- **No dating or "hook-up" apps:** Parents need to know who their kids are talking to. These apps prevent this. They also can easily open up the user to predators.
- **We will not use our phones to gossip or bully:** Cyber bullying is a hard thing to stop once it starts. Do not use any account to put down or demean any other person.

- **No abusive or inappropriate language communicated through this device:** Don't say anything online or through text messages that you wouldn't say in front of your grandma.
- **Handle phones legally (not while driving, etc.):** There are laws in almost every state prohibiting drivers from holding a phone in their hand while at the wheel. No distracted driving.
- **Respect the parameters of the family plan/data plan:** Parents pay for each phone's data plan each month. Don't abuse or go over your limit.
- **Be wise:** There are so many "rules" that can go into this category. But ultimately, the smartphone user has to use their brain and be smart with the gift (of a phone) that they hold in their hands.

This is your guide. You can edit these as you see fit for your situation. Here is Part 2 of 4 of the Family Phone Agreement.

FAMILY PHONE AGREEMENT - PART 2 OF 4

MORAL COMPASS: OUR NON-NEGOTIABLES

- Parents have full access to any phone at anytime.
- No sneaky apps designed to hide or keep secrets.
- Calls from parents are answered or responded to in a certain time period we decide.
- GPS location services are on for our family.
- No pornography and no sexting.
- No dating or "hook-up" apps.
- We will not use our phones to bully or gossip.
- No abusive or inappropriate language communicated through this device.
- Handle phones legally (not while driving, etc.).
- Respect the parameters of the family data plan.
- Be wise.

EXPERIENCE: TALK WITH A FRIEND

Your non-negotiables need to be exactly as you want them, but look, for all the firstborns[76] out there who are parents . . . take it easy! This agreement is a WIP . . . a work in progress. It will need to be adjusted as time goes on. However, the non-negotiables are **so important!** Talk with someone who really knows you and can give you good feedback on whether to add or subtract anything from this list.

[76] #Preach

29. Self-Awareness: Negotiables, Part 1

Previously, we covered non-negotiables, the plain ol' black-and-white. Now things get a little tougher, because over the next two chapters we will be doing the negotiables. This is where we "build our own fences." Your kid will experience complete freedom when they are grown up and out on their own. What they choose to do with that freedom is of supreme importance. Right now, you set the boundaries, through this Agreement with your kid. One day, your kid will have to do that for him- or herself.

The *non-negotiables* help build your kid's "fence" when it comes to things that are morally wrong. These *negotiable* rules, on the other hand, are for the areas that are gray. Think: Everything is permissible ... but not everything is beneficial (1 Corinthians 10:23). Your kid needs to learn how to be aware of how much freedom they can handle, and how to set boundaries to keep themselves within that realm. We call this self-awareness (knowing your triggers and limits) and self-governance (setting your own boundaries based on your self-awareness). In the next chapter we will cover self-governance, but first let's look at self-awareness.

SELF-AWARENESS

In order to set any kind of boundary, we need to *know* that a boundary needs to be made, and . . . where it should go. If you are self-aware of your screen time, you can limit it. If you are self-aware of your triggers and temptations on your phone, you can create boundaries to avoid them. If you are self-aware of the people around you physically, you can set aside your phone to engage with them. Self-awareness is the first step to controlling your behavior with your phone and setting boundaries.

As you become self-aware you begin to recognize triggers. A great way to start thinking about triggers is the acronym HALT. It stands for Hungry, Angry, Lonely, and Tired. You'd be surprised at how likely you are to make bad decisions when you are feeling one or multiple of those (hangry, anyone?!).

Again, the 8 Smartphone Domains chart is INCREDIBLY HELPFUL as you begin to become self-aware about your kid's smartphone. It shows all eight of the domains that we mentioned during Step 3 and some of the domains have incremental steps you could take in giving your kids more independence. Refer to the 8 Smartphone Domains at the end of this book or in Step Three.

So, how do you teach your kid to be self-aware? It will certainly take time as they mature. To begin building their self-awareness, you need to help them be aware of their habits. Someday they will notice these issues on their own, but for now, you are their "fence builder." And as you start down this journey some of your fences might need to metaphorically be large concrete retaining walls, others chain link, and some just chalk on the ground.

> *What type of fence do you need?*

An intentional conversation about what it means to be self-aware is where you should start, and that's exactly what this chapter's experience is! There's no addition to the Family Phone Agreement, as the next chapter's continuation of this conversation will fill in more of the contract. But for now, enjoy this experience.

EXPERIENCE: READ (OR WATCH) AND TALK!

Here's a fun exercise in self-awareness:

According to rsaeerch at Cmabrigde Uinervtisy, it deosn't mttaer in waht oredr the ltteers in a wrod are, the olny iprmoetnt tihng is taht the frist and lsat ltteer be at the rghit pclae. The rset can be a

> *toatl mses and you can sitll raed it wouthit porbelm. Tihs is bcuseae the huamn mnid deos not raed ervey lteter by istlef, but the wrod as a wlohe.*[77]

It's *amazing* what your mind can ignore! The example above shows a cool way your mind can ignore certain information so that it can comprehend the big picture. Try some awareness tests with your kid and see how observant you are![78] Use this as a starting point to ask them what it feels like to be *self-aware*. Also, enjoy some laughs at how much we can miss when we are not looking for it!

---

[77] This meme from 2003 is not technically true, as there is much more to our ability to read this paragraph than the paragraph itself explains. For the science behind why this works, check out axis.org/sanity-cambridge.

[78] Check out some of our favorite awareness test videos at axis.org/sanity-aware. Hilarious, interesting, and fun!

30. Self-Governance: Negotiables, Part 2

Time to dig into negotiables again! We know that this is not an easy or short conversation, so we hope that it continues through today and beyond! Boundaries are first built on self-awareness that identifies the need, and then, self-governance to create the "fence." Both are used in tandem for full freedom. This chapter is a continuation of last chapter's thoughts, focusing on building self-governance. Without self-governance, self-awareness is useless.

SELF-GOVERNANCE

Self-governance is really about self-control. At some point, we need to be able to govern our own habits so that we do not let our phones govern them for us. Do we own our phones or do they own us?

We just learned how essential self-awareness is in this process. But the next step is self-governance—setting limits on yourself to control your behavior. If no boundaries are placed, no behavior will change regardless of your self-awareness.

Self-governance is the natural follow-through of self-awareness. If you are aware you spend too much time on Instagram, but do nothing to govern that behavior, then what good was that self-aware thought?

The practice of self-governance will take time to develop, just like self-awareness. The boundaries you set for your kid will help them along this path. You are their self-awareness now, and the agreement is their self-governance. By setting boundaries for them now, you will teach them how to set boundaries on their own. As they learn where you limit their "negotiable" aspects—like money, location, time, internet, app store, texting, and social media—they will understand how to limit those things for themselves.

It is important to note that this is an incremental process.

Remember that the question, "When do I get my kid a phone," is the wrong question. This is not a 0 to 100 mph overnight process! Slowly you will let go more and more of your "governance" over to your kid. It's like going from 0 mph to 1 mph to 2 mph, etc. With growth and time, as your kid learns self-governance, they will be ready for more responsibility. So make sure you refer to the chart in Step Three that had incremental steps for the eight smartphone domains.

It is only through learning to set boundaries that a free life can be enjoyed fully. As you talk through these domains make sure your conversations are intentionally open on both sides (parent and child) and not just a verdict. Revisit past chapters for help in defining terms for one another, setting realistic expectations, or exploring options for more detailed questions about the app store, GPS, and sneaky apps.

> *Having a teenager living in your home, it's like having live-in tech support.*

And remember, unless you are an IT specialist, your children will have more expertise than you in many of these areas! Invite them into the process and ask them for advice on the setup if the trust is there!

Here is the next part of the Family Phone Agreement, including a section you will create on boundaries for full-fledged freedom:[79]

FAMILY PHONE AGREEMENT - PART 3 OF 4

SELF-AWARENESS & SELF-GOVERNANCE: JOURNEY OF TRUST WITH A DESTINATION OF INDEPENDENCE

Smartphones are complicated and families are different. Our family has agreed to follow the guidelines below. We are on a journey and this section of the agreement will change as technology and our family changes.

---

79 For the full Agreement, and an editable link, skip a few pages ahead.

Pick one or two guidelines per section.

	Parent Proposal	**Kid Proposal**
Money:		
Location:		
Time:		
Internet:		
App Store:		
Texting:		
Social Media:		

EXPERIENCE: PREPARE AND EXPLORE

This experience is mostly preparing for a future experience. In the future you will create the specific negotiable boundaries for the Family Phone Agreement. This means you will start a conversation with your family about what you want from their phones as well as what they want from your phone. This conversation will happen during your Family Phone Agreement Meeting, which will happen after you finish *Smartphone Sanity*.

Now you will start thinking about what you will write as negotiable boundaries for your kid in the contract (the Parent Proposal section of the Family Phone Agreement to the left).

When you have your Family Phone Agreement Meeting, you will all fill out this Family Phone Negotiables together, detailing how each person should handle their phone within the categories of Money, Time, Location, Internet, App Store, Texting, and Social Media; and for parents, Mirroring and Monitoring. Refer back to the previous chapters and decide what is best for you as a family. Remember, your kid gets to have a say in how you handle your phone—not just the other way around. Listen to these words from Dr. Kathy Koch:

> *The number one thing I hear from kids is that they wish their parents would put down their phones and pay attention to them.*

Don't let that heartbreaking statement be said in your home. Strong statements will be made (tinged with grace), lines will be drawn, and battles may ensue. It may not be that bad, but this is a good day to prepare for some disagreements about the standards children and parents have for smartphones.

This should be a conversation you invite your kid to join. They have ideas and opinions. Don't worry though, you still get the final say. Practice your I'm-not-shocked face and let your kid think about what rules might be best for THEM and for YOU.

Here are a couple examples to get the ball rolling. Your kid will be writing some of these so don't be shocked if they sting a little bit.

EXAMPLE KID'S PROPOSAL TO PARENTS:

1. Parents can't be on the phone from 6-8pm.
2. Do not have your phone in your face while talking to your children.
3. Parents will limit social media by checking social platforms only twice a day (OUCH!).
4. Parents will not "snoop" around on kid's phone.

EXAMPLE PARENT'S PROPOSAL TO KIDS:

1. Phones can't be in bedrooms or bathrooms.
2. Phones must be asleep (charging) after 9pm.
3. Children won't post on social media without parent approval and won't follow someone they don't know in real life.

Start thinking about what kind of guidelines you want to create,[80] and especially how you can approach the conversation with love and vulnerability.

[80]If you want to have some fun, there are Smartphone contracts all over the internet. Go to axis.org/sanity-examples to see: Basic, Snazzy, Family Agreement, Short 'n' Sweet, Check the Box, Funny Direct Mom, & Simple Signature.

“

Do we own our phones . . .

. . . or do
they own us?

”

31. Community: Forgiveness

This is the last section of the Family Phone Agreement! You are about to cross the finish line, and that is amazing! Remember, your family will be making a living, breathing agreement . . . and the goal is to see this as a journey to freedom. Use this Agreement to tell your kids that they are loved and that you want to guide them through this smartphone journey. Your family will not be perfect and everyone will make mistakes along the way. However, you will not allow this to be a single conversation but a regular conversation around the dinner table, driving home from school, and in your normal life. That's what *Smartphone Sanity* is about!

This is the final piece of the Family Phone Agreement. It's important to note: Technology WILL change. Sometimes these changes will give more control to parents and sometimes these changes will give more room for kids to sneak. That's why we will always need to lean into community.

COMMUNITY

What do we mean by community? Well, right now, you are your kid's community—their place where tough things can be discussed and guidance can be sought . . . and like we have mentioned many times before, *we are better in community than isolation.*

Why? Community gives us support, encouragement, accountability, and access to wisdom. You will always—God willing—be in community with your kid, but there will come a day when they will create community elsewhere. That is ok. In fact, it is great! However, you must teach your kid how to build community, because without it they will have no one to catch them when they fall.

By first creating a strong community within your family, you will teach them how to seek it out themselves. If you create an open, honest, and contempt-free relationship where they can truly tell you anything, then they will learn what community is all about. They will grow in vulnerability, trust, boundaries, and forgiveness. They will have practice reconciling when they have been wronged or when they offend. And one day when they are on their own they will have the experience needed to create and foster great community.

> *Your home is a contempt-free zone.*

Your family needs to have strong community because technology will change and mistakes will be made. Your kids will break the rules or find ways to sneak around your boundaries, or you will exasperate them and be unfair. You want to make sure that you remind them that you are there for them and eager to forgive them when they fall. They can tell you that they sought porn and feel trapped by it. They can tell you that they found a way to fool Screen Time. They can tell you that their friend is bullying others or if they were sent a sext. You have their back and this Family Phone Agreement is not about rules, but about flourishing as a family.

So, bottom line, *keep the conversation alive.* You will need to frequently revisit your Family Phone Agreement with your kid to keep the conversation open and growing. Continue to truly listen, and they will continue to talk. And always remind them that no matter what, *they can tell you anything.* Complete the Family Phone Agreement with Part 4:[81]

[81] For the full Agreement, and an editable link, skip a few pages ahead.

FAMILY PHONE AGREEMENT - PART 4 OF 4

COMMUNITY: YOU CAN TELL ME ANYTHING

Systems break, technology fails, and sometimes you will find a way around the rules. I need you to know that you can tell me *anything.* I want to know if you are being bullied online. I care about who you talk to and what you watch. If anyone finds a hole in the system and makes it known they will not be punished. Grace is a good thing and we are in this together!

EXPERIENCE: GO GIVE YOUR KID A HUG

That's it. Just give them a hug. A good one. Never fail to let them know that you love them, and they can tell you anything.

UNDER AUTHORITY: GOD

- Phones are Very Good, Cursed, & can be Redeemed.
- Since God owns everything, God owns all phones.

UNDER AUTHORITY: PARENTS

- As your parent, I am responsible to God as the ultimate steward of your phone when the phone is paid for by me and/or while you live in my home.
- You have no right to phone privacy.
- All passwords are accessible, including those for apps, & phones will be provided when asked for.
- We want to build your wisdom and restraint so one day you can be independent with your devices and not need oversight.

MORAL COMPASS: OUR NON-NEGOTIABLES

- Parents have full access to any phone at anytime.
- No sneaky apps designed to hide or keep secrets.
- Calls from parents are answered or responded to in a certain time period we decide.
- GPS location services are on for our family.
- No pornography and no sexting.
- No dating or "hook-up" apps.
- We will not use our phones to bully or gossip.
- No abusive or inappropriate language communicated through this device.
- Handle phones legally (not while driving, etc.).
- Respect the parameters of the family data plan.
- Be wise.

SELF-AWARENESS & SELF-GOVERNANCE: JOURNEY OF TRUST WITH A DESTINATION OF INDEPENDENCE

Smartphones are complicated and families are different. Our family has agreed to follow the guidelines below. We are on a journey and this section of the agreement will change as technology and our family changes.

Pick one or two guidelines per section.

	Parent Proposal	Kid Proposal
Money:		
Location:		
Time:		
Internet:		
App Store:		
Texting:		
Social Media:		

COMMUNITY: YOU CAN TELL ME ANYTHING

Systems break, technology fails, and sometimes you will find a way around the rules. I need you to know that you can tell me ***anything***. I want to know if you are being bullied online. I care about who you talk to and what you watch. If anyone finds a hole in the system and makes it known they will not be punished. Grace is a good thing and we are in this together!

ALWAYS REMEMBER:

This document is a living, breathing agreement. This is not made to punish. Our family sees this as a journey to freedom. One day you will leave our house and establish your own guidelines for living. You are loved and we want to guide you through this smartphone journey. Our family is not perfect and we will make mistakes along the way. We will not allow this to be a single conversation but a regular conversation around the dinner table, driving home from school, and in our normal life.

May you go into the world and use this smartphone to do good and not evil. May you be wise and be a light in the darkness. Use this technology to bring joy and redemption to others!

____________________________ ____________

Parent Name *Date*

____________________________ ____________

Kid Name *Date*

Axis.org/sanity-agreement has an editable version of this template.

33. Activity 4: Blessing

Wow! We did it! We made it to the end! You're now a smart phone family!!! Who you are in the present (experience), who you've been in the past (story), who you're becoming in the future (blessing) are all woven together to shape your identity. Each activity has leveraged the framework of experience, story, and blessing to influence your children in ways that will shape their identity and set them apart for God. This last activity is about blessing your kid. But what does that really look like?

Well, we think Malachi 4:6a has a beautiful description of what we believe to be blessing: "'. . . the hearts of fathers [will turn] to their children and the hearts of children to their fathers.'" This is an initiation by us as parents to turn our hearts toward our kids. And in turn, their response is to turn back towards us.

The second half of this verse says that if this "turning towards" doesn't happen, that the land will be cursed. Much of the pain and turmoil in the world today stems from this lack of turning our hearts toward each other. But imagine what would come of us turning our hearts towards our kids—and making a habit of it! What a blessing indeed!

Just a quick elaboration on the difference between blessing and encouragement . . . Encouragement actually means "to give heart." This is a situational response. We need to be given heart when we lack it. For example, your kid may be trying a team sport for the first time, or starting their first year of high school, or some other daunting task. They need your support telling them they have what it takes. This gives them strength; it gives them heart. It is a support from underneath.

Blessing, on the other hand, is a covering from above. Blessing first requires that we know the heart of our child, their stories, their character, their personality. Then, not only do we give them encouragement for the moment, but we begin to cast a vision for who they are to become. Note that this is not "You're going to become a great doctor/citizen/mother/athlete." That is all encouragement. Blessing is saying, "I know who God has created you to be through his image in you, and I can forecast into the future who I see you becoming and what I see you doing for God." Blessing is a vision of your child becoming who God really created them to be. It is knowing who they are today and giving them a vision of who they will become tomorrow. Tell them, "I know who you are, I see who you are, I am pleased with who you are, and I can envision a great future for you." Even Jesus needed this declaration in Mark 1:11b at his baptism: "'You are my beloved Son; with you I am well pleased.'"

What would happen in our families if we began to have that kind of perspective and that kind of language with our kids?! In the Scriptures, the word blessing actually means, "to kneel." What if we knelt before our kids, blessing them in this holy way? Is this something you could do once? Could you do this on a regular basis?

> *In the Scriptures, the word blessing actually means "to kneel."*

What you choose to say in your blessing doesn't need to be heavy handed or forced . . . but it does have to be tied to their very being, as someone created in the image of God. In that case, you are not saying, "You're doing good," but instead, "You are gifted in this way that God has made you." So, be aware of their loves and talents and start to think about how they reflect the image of our good God. Consider kneeling before them, and may you turn your heart towards your kid as they turn their heart to you.

EXPERIENCE: ACTIVITY 4!

The fourth activity of *Smartphone Sanity* is all about blessing your kid. We hope you'll take advantage of this opportunity! Providing an intentional blessing to your kid is one of the most impactful things that any parent can experience. And, it will be impactful for your kid, too. This activity is meant to draw you closer to each other and to God through recognizing and bestowing a blessing. Remember to set aside time in your schedule for Activity 4! There are three options for this experience. Do whichever you have time for!

1. Look, I'm Busy
2. You Can Do It!
3. The Overachiever Edition

WHAT'S THE ACTIVITY?

Experience: Eating a family meal together.
Story: Enter into your family story.
Blessing: Prepare a blessing to read over your kid.

Here's How It Works: You (the parents) provide an intentional blessing over your kid. The best situation for this would be in front of the whole family. The goal during this time is for your kid to be verbally blessed in an intentional way by a parent. It will feel awkward to think about, but this could truly be one of the most special moments you've experienced as a parent. Embrace this with no agenda, but to simply bestow your blessing upon your kid. You'll be glad you did.

OPTION 1: LOOK, I'M BUSY.

Step 1 and Done: Grab a bucket of fried chicken. Eat it with your kids. Bless them.

OPTION 2: YOU CAN DO IT!

Step 1: *Plan a 1-2 hour window in your calendar* where you plan a special family meal for all parents and children, and to give your kid a blessing.
Step 2: *Plan the meal.* The meal should be in a private place. This is really important. We recommend a unique location in your home (like a fire pit, or other new location) or someplace like a park. We think outdoor

locations are typically best for flipping the script to make this a memorable experience. We discourage choosing a public restaurant setting because blessing your kid is a very intimate experience and you will want no distractions or interruptions. **Food Tip**: To make things easy, order take-out from a family-favorite restaurant. This is worth the financial investment and makes for simple meal preparation and cleanup so you can fully focus on the blessing.

Step 3: *Write out a personalized blessing from each parent to each kid.* You'll read this blessing to your kid. Writing it out ahead of time will ensure that it's intentional and fully thought out (we don't recommend "winging it" with blessings). A blessing related to your kid's smartphone use can be done, but is not required (remember, no agenda!). Here is a reminder of what blessing means from our overview of Experience, Story, and Blessing at the beginning of *Smartphone Sanity*:

> ***Blessing****, as a verb, does not refer to providing material provision, but instead to pointing out the image of God in someone. Calling that out and naming it blesses that person's unique future in God's plan.*

Note that this is different from encouragement. Encouragement focuses on what they have done or are doing. Blessing affirms who they are. In that case, you are not saying "**You're doing good**," but instead, "**<u>You are</u>** gifted in this way that God has made you." As you write the blessing think of the "glory" of the person that you're blessing. Bless who they are, not what they do. Think upon their giftedness. What comes to mind?

> *"Bless who they are, not what they do."*

Step 4: *Eat the meal and give your blessing to each kid.* Transition into the blessing time by talking about the smartphone experience you've had with this book. Tell your kid you've been thinking about their giftedness and strengths while going through the growth-spurt of this training. Because of this recent reflection, you want to bless your kid by reading them what you wrote down. When giving the blessing it's okay to read your blessing, but make eye contact with your kid. It's a great idea to give them the written version of the blessing afterwards. Just make sure you bless them verbally first.

Tip: To show them how important this is to you, place your hand on their shoulder or even consider kneeling before them during the blessing. This is a sacred thing, naming the glory of God in your kid. Show them that!

OPTION 3: OVERACHIEVER EDITION

Steps 1-2: Same instructions as Option 2.

Step 3: Same instructions as Option 2. **Additionally,** write and prepare a special blessing for your spouse during this time as well. This can be healing and helpful for you too! And, let's be real, we're still working on becoming who God made us to be, too!

Step 4: Same instructions as Option 2. **Additionally,** give your kid a gift or object to signify the blessing. It should be something that would remind them of what you say in your blessing, not some gift they've been wanting. Make it stand out, and make them remember this time!

May these instructions help you bless your kid in a powerful way! If you have any questions or confusions—or stories to share—feel free to reach out to us at axis.org. We want to engage in this special time with you!

We can't wait to hear from you on how your activity goes, and as always, we would love it if you would share your stories with us at axis.org. May this blessing activity truly bless you and your kid!

END

34. Family Phone Agreement Meeting

You made it to the end of *Smartphone Sanity*! YAY!

FINAL EXPERIENCE: FAMILY PHONE AGREEMENT MEETING

The Family Phone Agreement Meeting is the culmination of all the work you've done throughout reading this book. If you've done the activities and experiences, or even if you have just educated yourself by reading, you now have a holistic perspective on the smartphone and how your family interacts with it. You've also had the opportunity to start meaningful conversations with your kid. The key to the family meeting is that it's a *two-way conversation*.

Use the Family Phone Agreement as a template to reverse engineer what to discuss at the Family Phone Agreement Meeting. You're now ready to have this meeting and for it to be a successful conversation. Use the Family Phone Agreement Meeting as the BEGINNING, not the end, of the Family Phone Agreement process.

WHAT'S THE ACTIVITY?

Experience: Meet and create your Family Phone Agreement.
Story: Honestly share about your and others' phone use.
Blessing: Bless them and affirm,"You can tell me anything."

Schedule a family meeting to discuss what you've learned during *Smartphone Sanity* and discuss the components of the Family Phone Agreement. This meeting can look however you'd like. Planning around food and in a unique space/place like the other activities would be beneficial. Don't forget to use experience, story, and blessing in your approach to smartphone communication as you continue to lead your kid to growth and maturity.

Tip: *Make sure this meeting is conversational not dictatorial.* It's better if you communicate this meeting as the time to discuss the agreement as opposed to unveiling what you (the parent) have already decided. It's okay to present a "rough draft" and go from there. The Family Phone Agreement is a template that you can build upon. As we've said in the Family Phone Agreement, it's best to view it as a living document. This means that you should customize it as much as you can. Include specific aspects of your family in it to make it your own. Remember that it is a **Family** Phone Agreement—this means that the **whole family** contributes to making it, and its boundaries apply to the **whole family**!

We hope you've gotten a lot out of your *Smartphone Sanity* experience, and hope you're excited to have this family meeting with all the intentional, prayerful preparation you've done leading up to it.

35. The Most Important Conversation

As you reflect on this book, we hope it encourages you to be a smartphone missionary to your kid. By the grace of God and the guidance of the Holy Spirit, *seek* to reach into their world, just like Jesus did for all of humanity.

This may mean limiting your freedom for a season to join them in a technology fast, or it may mean giving up your phone privacy to lead by example and show that you have nothing to hide. It could also mean downloading Snapchat (or whatever their go-to app is) simply to understand what they love about it.

Being a missionary will always mean empathizing and being curious enough to try to understand their reality—a reality where bullying not only happens in person, but also online 24/7; where male/female has never been a given, but an ambiguous spectrum; where their identity feels like it's dependent on "likes," and where sexting is an expected part of dating. *You have what it takes, we believe in you, and your kid needs you!*

Hold fast to your heart connection with your kid, and hold fast to the *one conversation* that lasts a lifetime. That *one conversation* is the most important conversation you will ever have with your kid.

As April said at the beginning of the book, "I've only had *one conversation* with my dad, and we have never stopped having that *one conversation*."

Materials and Resources

Here are just a few handy tools for you to navigate the content in this book. First there is a **Link Quick Guide** to all the links mentioned in this book, chronologically.

Next we've made a handy graphic attempting to lay out and organize the different aspects of the smartphone conversations we call the **Smartphone Conversation Matrix**. It might help you visualize and work through the material in *Smartphone Sanity*, or function as a good refresher upon picking this book back up.

Finally, we have included the charts from Steps Three and Four for quick reference. These cover the **8 Domains of the Smartphone**, and levels of control for each domain.

As always, feel free to contact us at support@axis.org or chat with us at axis.org with questions, comments, stories, or problems!

Link Quick Guide

axis.org/ct	*Free! Culture Translator sign-up*
axis.org/guides	*All Axis Parent Guides*
axis.org/sanity-email	*Email copy and paste*
axis.org/sanity-pencil	*Awesome pencil video*
axis.org/sanity-jelly	*"I am a Jelly Donut!" ~JFK*
axis.org/sanity-drpowell	*Dr. Powell Video on "warmth"*
axis.org/sanity-growth	*Growth Mindset video*
axis.org/sanity-trap	*Don't do it. It's a trap . . .*
axis.org/sanity-groove	*Inspirational mullet dance*
axis.org/sanity-snapchat	*Free Parent's Guide to Snapchat*
axis.org/sanity-wisdom	*Bible Project video on Proverbs*
axis.org/sanity-addiction	*Video on phones & slot machines*
axis.org/sanity-dope	*Stats for dopamine studies*
axis.org/sanity-hacked	*Video on Instagram hacking*
axis.org/sanity-connection	*TED talk about addiction*
axis.org/sanity-tripledogdareyou	*A Christmas Story iconic line*
axis.org/sanity-shame	*Dr. Brown & Dr. Allender videos*
axis.org/sanity-danger	*Stats for Five Pathologies*
axis.org/sanity-sexting	*Free Parent's Guide to Sexting*
axis.org/sanity-pregnant	*Funniest. Video. Ever.*
axis.org/sanity-ben	*Spiderman pep-talk*
axis.org/sanity-catfish	*Scary video about predators*
axis.org/sanity-protect	*Protect Young Eyes set-up*
axis.org/sanity-email2	*Another email copy and paste*
axis.org/sanity-subway	*NYC subways—gross*
axis.org/sanity-smash	*Parent's smashing kid's tech*
axis.org/sanity-social	*Free Social Media Conversation Kit*
axis.org/sanity-cambridge	*Cambridge study*
axis.org/sanity-aware	*Awesome awareness tests*
axis.org/sanity-examples	*Sample phone contracts*
axis.org/sanity-agreement	*Axis editable phone agreement!*

Smartphone Conversation Matrix 1.0

Remember the first chapter called "The Catastrophe that Caused this Book" where the student in my youth group said, "The stricter the parent the sneakier the child?" I vividly remember that moment. I felt so defeated and I made a vow to solve the smartphone riddle. Over the next few weeks, I took my Thursdays at Axis to work offsite in my church's basement with a trusty whiteboard. My initial goal was to outline all the potential conversations surrounding the smartphone. Here is the original whiteboard:

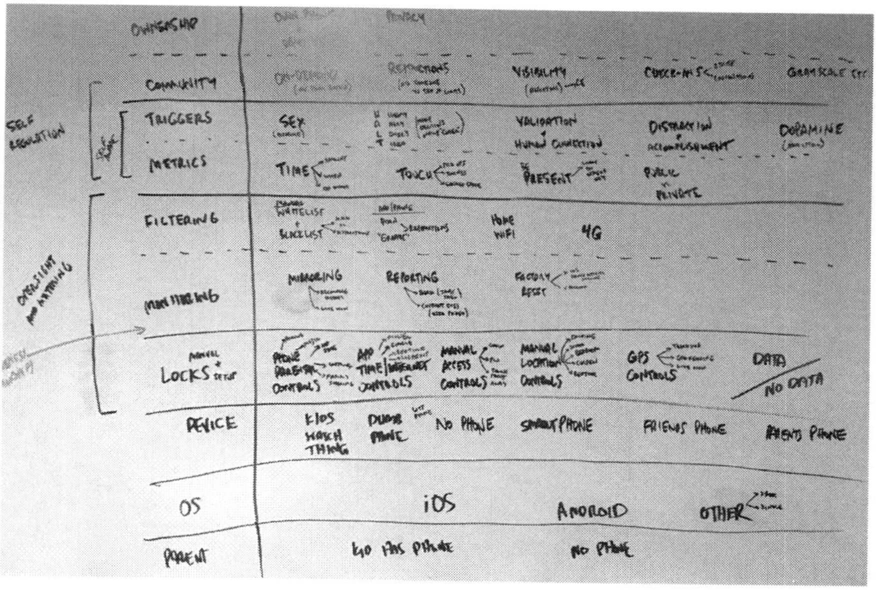

Smartphone Conversation Matrix 2.0

Many conversations later . . . here is the current version!

Teen Ownership	Our world is very good & cursed. How can you redeem it as a person?	God owns the phone & your kid stewards their phone.	Although your kid has privacy they choose to be in community.
Maturity	Restrictions: asking a friend to set limits behind a passcode.	Limits: limiting that "app," distractions, grayscale, notifications.	Visibility: reporting to friends your phone actions. CovenantEyes.
Triggers	Human Connection.	Validation.	Distraction.
Metrics & Mindset	Time: amount, when, & on what.	Touch: pick-ups, touches, & notifications.	Sacred Space: when are you without your phone?
Filtering	Home WiFi OpenDNS settings on routers.	Native Phone Restrictions: whitelist & blacklist websites.	Native Phone Restrictions: limit adult content.
Monitoring	Very Manual: App discipleship especially with social media.	Manual: checking phones randomly.	Mirroring: from another device for texting & apps.
Parental Controls	Main Login: AppleID or Google Login & Password.	Family Sharing: Ask to Buy, download, update, & in-app purchases.	Native Restrictions: Internet, Apps, & Location.
Manual Controls	Parent has logins, passcode, & passwords for everything.	At home policies: homework, meals, bedroom, & bathroom.	Away policies: school, church, car, friend's homes.
Non-Negotiables	Parent has access to phone/apps at any time & can install software.	Parent checks phone frequently & knows about apps (finsta . . .).	No sneaky apps, secrets, hidden accounts, changing pw.
Current State	No phone yet.	Sibling currently has a phone.	Your kid currently has a phone.
Agreement	No agreement, phone was given in the box it came in. Yikes!	No written agreement but a verbal agreement.	Written agreement from parents.
Relationship	People matter! The phone is a servant not a master!	Open, trust based relationship filled with warmth & celebration.	More positives than criticisms.
Parent's Marriage	Married parents.	Divorced parents.	Remarried parents.
Data Plan	No WiFi & No Data (LTE).	WiFi Only.	WiFi & Data (LTE).
Device	Friend's phone.	No phone.	Parent's phone.
Operating System	iOS.	Android.	Other.
Parent Ownership	Our world is very good & cursed. How can we redeem it as a family?	God owns the phone. Parents steward phone. Kid uses the phone.	Kid has no right to phone privacy from parents.

Kid buys their phone from you & buys data plan.	Kid pays for cases, accessories.	Kid pays for phone if/when it breaks.	If kid still lives at home, parent has limited access to phone.	If your child ever needs help you are always there with open arms.
On-Demand: panic button with your community.	Scheduled: check-ins with your community.	See rTribe app.		
Accomplishment.	Habits & Dopamine Addiction.	Sex Impulse & Pleasure.	Hungry, Angry, Lonely, & Tired.	Make boundary decisions while "sober."
Bedtime: where does your phone sleep & are you sleeping?	Philosophy of Presence: decided by those with you.	Under Authority: who have you invited to check-in with you?	Privacy: is there anything on phone you don't want others to see?	Moral Compass, Self-Aware, Self-Govern, & in Community.
Native Phone Restrictions: see system parental controls below.	CovenantEyes filters only in their browser app.			
Manual: Teensafe.com or uKnowChilds.com for $15/mo.	Auto: Bark.us will automatically monitor & report to you. $9/mo.	Auto: CovenantEyes will monitor porn found on phones.		
Native Restrictions: media ratings, porn, blacklisting.	Screen Time App - for screen time awareness.	Screen Time App - time limits, PM to AM tech curfew, & screen control.	Notifications, Do Not Disturb, & Emergency Bypass.	
Friend policies: when friends are over & with friend's devices.	Phone location at night.	Phone Discipline: taking phone away & removing functionality.	Amnesty, Forgiveness, & Relationship.	
Agreed family response times to calls & texts.	GPS location services are always on.	No porn, sexting, online dating or "hook-up" apps.	No bullying, or inappropriate (abusive) language.	No illegal actions including driving laws about phones, etc.
Written agreement made with your kids' input.	Agreement Part 1: Ownership & Privacy.	Agreement Part 2: Non-Negotibles.	Agreement Part 3: Negotiables.	Agreement Part 4: Trust, Grace, & Forgiveness.
Consistently affirming your love & desire for their best interest.	Leading by example & pursuing a growth mindset.	Safe to confess to, because you are fair & won't over react.	Safe because you won't shame them.	Discipline is NOT indefinite or punitive.

The Smartphone Conversation Matrix

Limited phone, typically designed for younger kids.	Dumb Phone, or Gabb Wireless Phone.	iPad/Tablet or iPod Touch.	iPod touch.	Smartphone.
Parent decides who buys the phone.	Parent decides who pays for the data plan.	Parent decides how much data is allowed per person.	Parent decides who pays for cases & accessories.	Parent decides who pays for phone if it breaks.

The 8 Smartphone Domains

1. Non-Negotiables

No more non-negotiables.

- No illegal actions including driving laws about phones, etc.
- No bullying, or inappropriate (abusive) language.
- No porn, sexting, online dating, or "hook-up" apps.
- GPS location services are always on.
- Agreed family response times to calls & texts.
- No sneaky apps, hidden accounts, changing passwords, & no secrets.
- Parent will check phone frequently & know about every app.
- Parent has access to phone/apps at any time, has passcode, all passwords & logins, & can install software. There is no right to phone privacy.
- Phones are very good, cursed, & can be redeemed. God owns everything, & He owns all phones. Parents are responsible to God as the ultimate steward of the family phones.

2. Money

Your kid pays for everything.

- Who pays for the phone if/when it breaks?
- Who pays for phone cases & accessories?
- Who pays for apps, streaming music services, etc.
- Who pays for the phone plan & data?
- Who buys the phone? How often can it be upgraded?

3. Location

No policies for location.

<u>*Policies while Away:*</u>

- Friend's Homes
- Car
- Church
- School

<u>*Policies for Home:*</u>

- Sleeping
- Homework
- Meals
- Bathroom/Shower
- Bedroom

4. Time

No limits on time.

- Notification setup to minimize distractions.
- Scheduled downtime from phone.
- Specific app time limits.
- Total phone time limits.
- Tech Curfew PM to AM.
- Screen Time & Family Link. Native phone screen time control apps.
- Screen Time & Family Link. Native phone screen time awareness apps.

5. Internet	6. App Store	7. Texting	8. Social Media
	Allow App Store.		
	No "Family Sharing." No deleting apps setting. Limit adult content setting.		*Allow Social Media.*
Allow native browser & App Store browsers.	No "Family Sharing." No deleting apps setting. Limit adult content setting. Restrict apps based on ratings.		Multiple Social Media. Use Bark.us. Follow them & don't be a weirdo.
Allow native browser. Turn on "limit adult content" in settings. No App Store browsers.	App Store with "Family Sharing" WITHOUT "Ask to Buy." No deleting apps setting. Limit adult content setting. Restrict apps based on ratings.	*Allow texting.*	Allow multiple social media. Approve posts initially. Approve who they want to follow. Know login & password. Follow them but don't interact publicly. Login on occasion & look around. Use Bark.us.
Allow native browser with whitelisted or blacklisted sites. On Android use "approve sites." Turn on "limit adult content" in settings. No App Store because of browsers.	App Store with "Family Sharing" & "Ask to Buy." No deleting apps setting. Limit adult content setting.	Allow texting. Frequently monitor manually. Definitely pay for Bark.us reporting software. Bark will see deleted texts.	Same as below except require approval for fewer posts.
No native browser. Install & pay for Covenant Eyes browser. Turn on filtering & reporting. Turn on "limit adult content" in settings. No App Store because of 3rd party browsers.	Always know every app on their phone.	Allow texting. Mirror texts on a separate device or consider paying for a monitoring service like TeenSafe. Frequently monitor manually. Definitely pay for Bark.us reporting software.	Allow one social media. Approve all posts. Approve everyone they want to follow. Know login & password. Follow them but don't interact publicly. Login on occasion & look around. Use Bark.us.
No native browser & no App Store for other browsers.	No App Store.	No texting.	No Social Media.

About Axis

Axis was born the year the smartphone was born.

When it comes to the next generation, so much has changed in the last decade. Actually, even in the *last month*. Do you know what the eggplant emoji really means? Do you like Skywalker? Have you ever Netflixed and chilled? Does your daughter know Ana, Mia, Deb, and Sue?[82] Have you hired a Fortnite coach for your kid so he (or she!) can get a piece of the $30M prize? Have you ever wondered why the next generation is NOT eager to get their driver's licenses on their 16th birthday, often waiting until they are 18 or 19 years old? Have you had a conversation about LGBTQQIP2SAA[83] with a teenager? *Ok, we just tried to overwhelm you a little.*

The rising generation is awesome. But as with every emerging generation, the rules of the game have changed. Same hormones, same peer-pressure, same annoying standardized tests at school. But, now there is Snapchat, and smartphones, and spectrums for gender, and eSports, and a spike in teen anxiety, and . . . whatever that new app is . .

The good news is that parents (and grandparents) have what it takes to reach their kids (and grandkids), and Axis exists to make parents' lives easier by making their conversations with their teens deeper and more frequent.

The magic of Axis is Culture Translation: We interpret student trends for parents as well as translate timeless theology, philosophy, and essential questions of life for their teens.

Since 2007 Axis teams have spoken face to face with over 240,000 teenagers, and every year we reach thousands more. Our live-speaking teams are a research engine that allows us to have our finger on the pulse of teen culture so we can create digital resources that equip over 136k parents every month. Every year Axis helps hundreds of thousands of caring adults have millions of conversations with their 8- to 18-year-olds *that they would not have started without Axis.*

Axis connects the wisdom of parents with the wonder of their kids.

---

[82] Ana = Anorexia, Mia = Bulimia, Deb = Depression, and Sue = Suicidal Ideation or Suicide. All are common hashtags.

[83] Lesbian, Gay, Bisexual, Transgender, Queer, Questioning, Intersex, Pansexual, Two Spirit, Asexual, Ally, etc. Tumblr has 100+ options.

Axis Resources

The Axis Culture Translator email reaches 46,000+ people a week and helps parents stay on top of student ***trends***. Axis Parent Guides on 90+ ***topics*** offer a deep dive in 10 pages or less. Axis convenes a yearly online Parenting Summit that features interviews from 50 parenting expert ***teachers***. Axis video Conversation Kits tackle tough ***themes*** that parents must address with their students, like porn, drugs, anxiety, social media, and gender.

Axis has also developed content on the toughest challenge facing parents today: their teen's ***smartphone***. Axis helps parents set up their teen's phone for success by balancing reasonable boundaries *while simultaneously* creating an atmosphere of trust. Axis has created *Reclaiming the Smartphone: Four Essential Smartphone Conversations* and the *30-Day Smartphone Family Reboot*. The book you're holding right now is the latest in this endeavor, the journey to *Smartphone Sanity*.

About the Authors

DAVID EATON

David Eaton is the President of Axis, which he cofounded with Jeremiah Callihan in 2007. David[84] has spoken with over 100,000 students & parents and now spends his time finding new ways for Axis to reach more families.

David has led partnerships between Axis and Family Life Today, MOPS, Young Life, Youth for Christ, Focus on the Family, Ravi Zacharias International Ministries, the Association of Christian Schools International, Compassion International, Word of Life, Moody Radio, The Colson Center, Care-Net, and many, many others.

David is married to his intelligent and creative wife Lindsey, and they have three kids: Shiloh Abigail, Zion Daniel, and Vale Calvary. The Eatons live in Colorado.

---

[84] David rarely enjoys speaking in 3rd person.

JEREMIAH CALLIHAN

As CEO and Cofounder of Axis, Jeremiah leads the vision, strategy, product development, and execution of the plan to reach as many families as possible with the Gospel. It's Jeremiah's passion to equip caring adults to be the best possible missionaries and spiritual guides to the next generation. Seeing lifetime conversations between parents and their kids which leads to life-long faith in Jesus is what motivates Jeremiah every day.

Jeremiah lives in Colorado and has been married 15 years to his best friend, Kim. They're in the midst of *one conversation* with each of their four amazing kids. When he isn't playing catch or board games or on the trampoline with his kids, he might be eating french toast, playing basketball, watching football, or reading a great book somewhere outside with inspirational music in the background.

RESTORATION PROJECT

Restoration Project is an amazing ministry for men to fully engage as fathers, husbands, and brothers. They have an awesome rite of passage program for fathers and their sons and daughters. They were instrumental in the creation of the activities in this book. Greg, Jesse, and Chris . . . we respect you and are grateful for your mission. Check out restorationproject.net.

About the Editor

SARAH MILES

Sarah Miles is the owner of Kiln Literary, an editing company dedicated to aiding writers with their creative endeavors, be it a small article or a magnum opus. She provides a creative sounding board, suggestions and proofing, or full editing services, depending on the author's needs. Sarah works with a whole range of authors—non-fiction, creative non-fiction, fiction, fantasy fiction, and anything in-between. Notable examples include *Church Without Walls, Girl on Purpose,* and *The Salesperson Paradox.* Find out more at kilnliterary.com or email sarah@kilnliterary.com.

Sarah lives in beautiful Colorado with her husband, Woodson. They love to take walks outside, discuss what makes a good story, and enjoy time with their friends. Sarah's bookcase is stacked two or three books deep, and she has a corner of her kitchen dedicated to tea. She could be called a typical bookworm.

Acknowledgements

We are grateful to the Axis Team and the Axis Board. You are awesome and you inspire us. Thank you for helping us make this book a reality. You helped us dream, brainstorm, collect stories, research, and organize this book! You are the best.

Thank you to Sarah Miles who was long-suffering, thoughtful, and an incredible advocate for this book. You are a wonderful sounding board and editor. And Rob, thanks for the Thai lunch that opened this providential door.

To our wives and kids . . . we are in this together! Special thanks to Lindsey Eaton for helping polish the final manuscript for grammar and tone!

Finally, thank you to the families who let us share parts of your smartphone story. Bob, Craig, Bill, Lynne, Belinda, April#1, Penny, Alexandra, April#2, Dan the Man, Scott, Harper, Gregg, Lisa, Christin, Randy, John, Airplane Lady, Sarah, "Darby," Sandy, Dr. Eaton, and that mom from North Carolina.

Finally, there are so many amazing thought leaders who have influenced Axis over the years. We are standing on the shoulders of giants.

Made in the
USA
Columbia, SC

79200265R00135